WHEN MIGHT BECOMES
HUMAN RIGHT

WHEN MIGHT BECOMES BECOMES HUMAN RIGHT

Essays on Democracy and the
Crisis of Rationality

Janne Haaland Matláry

GRACEWING

First published in 2006 as *Veruntreute Menschenrechte. Droht eine Diktatur des Relativismus?* By Sankt Ulrich Verlag, Augsburg

This edition published in 2007

Gracewing
2 Southern Avenue
Leominster
Herefordshire HR6 0QF

ISBN 0 85244 031 6
ISBN 978 0 85244 031 5

Typeset by Action Publishing Technology Ltd,
Gloucester GL1 5SR

CONTENTS

ABBREVIATIONS

CEO	Chief Executive Officer
COE	Council of Europe
CSR	Corporate Social Responsibility
ECHR	European Convention on Human Rights (also European Court of Human Rights)
ECJ	European Court of Justice
EU	European Union
ICBL	International Campaign to Ban Landmines
MFA	Minister for Foreign Affairs
NATO	North Atlantic Treaty Organization
NGO	Non-governmental organization
OECD	Organization for Economic Cooperation and Development
OSCE	Organization for Security and Cooperation in Europe
PC	Political correctness
SOP	Standard operating procedure
UDHR	Universal Declaration of Human Rights
UN	United Nations
UNSC	United Nations Security Council
WHO	World Health Organization
WMD	Weapon of Mass Destruction
WTO	World Trade Organization

ACKNOWLEDGEMENTS

Ever since I was a *Gymnasiumschuler* I have been interested in the question of ethics and politics; more precisely in the question of whether there can be any *Fester Punkt* beyond positivist law and majority opinion. This is naturally the question of the *Rechtsstaat*, of whether basic values in a constitution or in a human rights convention are really beyond the reach of the vagaries of public opinion and political correctness. The need to find an answer to this question led me both to my field of study, political science, and eventually to the Catholic Church and her doctrine of natural law. In Thomism I found the continuation of the Aristotelian rational tradition of politics as the pursuit of the common good – *summum bonum* – through reason.

Over the years this preoccupation of mine has led to several essays, articles, and talks in various European contexts. In this book I present a number of them in a revised form together with some new chapters that together will hopefully contribute to the European debate over relativism, human rights, and majority tyranny. This is the most important debate we conduct in our democracies today; and one where the natural law tradition of the Church seems to offer the only position 'in the market' which argues that ethics and reason belong together.

Christianity is the religion of the word – *Logos* – that is, of rationality. It builds on the classical notion of the rational as particular to the human being; as that which sets it apart from animals. Aristotle defines the human being as

a 'rational and social being', where rationality means the
ability to reason about ethics, about right and wrong.
Animals, he points out, also have language, but they
cannot reason. To reason implies to speak in the language
of universals, which is the language of ethics and *therefore*
the language of law and politics: 'Stealing is wrong and
should be forbidden' means that stealing is wrong for each
human being, everywhere and always. The law is the
proper instrument to use to forbid it. But if I say that
'sailing is good for everyone and should be prescribed', I
speak nonsense because I speak about a particular, private
interest – of mine, but not something that concerns the
summum bonum of society. In the use of language we
immediately recognize that the argument about stealing is
sound, but that the argument about sailing is illogical.
Thus, we are born with the ability to rationalize ethical
questions.

   I am convinced that we have to rediscover these essen-
tials of politics and law in order to preserve what may be
left of the *Rechtsstaat* in Europe. Today human rights have,
rightly so, become the new political 'Bible', but a profound
relativism regarding basic values prevails. Human rights
move the *Rechtsstaatproblematik* to the international level,
where no political apparatus exists in the form of 'checks
and balances'. This complicates matters further, while
there at the same time reigns a strong degree of relativism
regarding what these human rights constitute.

   This book pleads for a return *ad fontes*, to the classical
rationalism of ancient political thought. This tradition,
called natural law, has to this day been especially well
preserved in the Catholic Church. It is not specifically
Christian, but the Christian view of the human being
(*Menschenwurde*) is different from the classical one. I think
we have to rediscover and modernize natural law in order
to ensure that democracy does not become majority – or as
it may be, minority tyranny. In order to succeed in this, we
have to focus on two themes: one, being willing to
acknowledge that the central political question today,
when we debate human rights, is not the concept of *right*

but the concept of *human*; and two, being willing to re-examine what rationality means. The latter is today almost exclusively regarded as a matter of pursuing one's own material interests, but this is a very impoverished view of rationality. Instead rationality must be returned to in its classical form, emanating from a human being who is able to reason about ethics and therefore, about politics and law.

During ten years of sometime diplomatic service for the Holy See I had occasion to study and participate in the 'human rights diplomacy' of Pope John Paul II. I was impressed by the fact that he developed and applied the notion of human dignity in international politics, through his encyclicals, speech, and action. No other actor on the world scene did that; representing the continuation of the natural law tradition of the Church, which is a general, 'non-religious' sphere of thought proper to politics. The Vatican spokesman Dr Navarro-Valls suggested that I should write a book on the importance of human dignity and human rights in current politics.

My long-standing interest in this theme naturally led me to Joseph Cardinal Ratzinger. His writings on rationality, freedom and the 'tyranny of relativism' in modern democracy are incisive and radical. I discussed the idea for a book with him in several meetings in the Vatican, and he made suggestions for readings and even supplied a bibliography from his own hand. He also graciously offered to write the introduction to this book; an offer which naturally could not stand when he was elected Pope in April 2005.

I remain tremendously grateful for his interest and equally inspired by his pen. If there is one person that fulfils the criteria of classical rationality, it is he.

Janne Haaland Matláry

PREFACE

Mary Ann Glendon

In this fascinating collection of essays, Janne Haaland Matláry explores one of the most troubling political questions of our time: how can 'human rights' serve as a universal common standard in a political climate where relativism prevails? Where the scope and meaning of every right is hotly contested? If human rights cannot be placed on a solid philosophical basis, the doors are open for endless manipulation and deconstruction. The hopes they represent – for democracy, rule of law, peace, and dignified living – dissolve amidst power politics. And might becomes right.

Some of the most profound thinkers of the late twentieth century had already called attention to the risks of resting a noble enterprise on shaky foundations. Pope John Paul II, for example, was a great admirer of the 1948 Universal Declaration of Human Rights, describing it as 'one of the highest expressions of human conscience of our time' and 'a real milestone on the path of the moral progress of humanity'.[1] But in the fateful year of 1989, he warned that the document 'does not present *the anthropological and ethical foundations of the human rights* which it proclaims'.[2] A few years after the fall of communism in

---

[1] John Paul II, 'Address to the United Nations', 2 October 1979, par. 7, and 'Address to the United Nations', 5 October 1995, par. 2.

[2] John Paul II, 'Address to the Diplomatic Corps Accredited to the Holy See', 9 January 1989, par. 7.

Eastern Europe, the Nobel prize-winning poet Czeslaw Miloscz put the dilemma even more sharply. Evoking 'those beautiful and deeply moving words which pertain to the old repertory of the rights of man and the dignity of the person', Miloscz wrote: 'I wonder at this phenomenon because maybe underneath there is an abyss ... How long will they stay afloat if the bottom is taken out?'[3]

One might well wonder how it happened that such an imposing edifice as the 1948 Declaration was constructed with so little attention to foundations. The fact is that the fathers and mothers of the post-Second World War human rights project were well aware of the omission. They just didn't have time to remedy it. When the UN's first Human Rights Commission, chaired by Eleanor Roosevelt, began to draft a 'bill of rights' to which persons of all nations and cultures could subscribe, they were immediately faced with two problems: no one really knew whether there were any such common principles, or what they might be. Anticipating those difficulties, UNESCO had asked a group of philosophers (some well known in the West like Jacques Maritain and others from Confucian, Hindu and Muslim cultures) to look into the matter.

The philosophers sent a questionnaire to leading thinkers all over the world, from Mahatma Gandhi to Teilhard de Chardin, and in due course, they reported that, somewhat to their surprise, there were a few common standards of decency that were widely shared, though not always formulated in the language of rights. They pronounced themselves 'convinced that the members of the United Nations share common convictions on which human rights depend'.[4] At the same time, however, they cautioned that 'those common convictions are stated in terms of different philosophic principles and

3   Czeslaw Miloscz, 'The Religious Imagination at 2000', *New Perspectives Quarterly* (Fall 1997), p. 32.
4   UNESCO, *Human Rights: Comments and Interpretations*, Wingate, London, 1949, pp. 268–71.

on the background of divergent political and economic systems'.

The UNESCO group's bottom line was that agreement could be reached across cultures concerning certain rights that 'may be seen as implicit in man's nature as an individual and as a member of society and to follow from the fundamental right to live'.[5] But they harboured no illusions about how deep that agreement went. As Maritain famously put it, when someone asked him how consensus had been achieved among such diverse informants: 'We agree about the rights but on condition no one asks us why!'[6]

Maritain and his colleagues did not view that problem as fatal to proceeding. For the time being, he maintained, the only feasible goal was to reach agreement 'not on the basis of common speculative ideas, but on common practical ideas'.[7] Since there was consensus that some things are so terrible in practice that no one will publicly approve them, and some things are so good in practice that virtually no one will openly oppose them, a common project could go forward, even in the absence of agreement on the reasons for those positions. That practical consensus, the UNESCO philosophers said, was enough 'to enable a great task to be undertaken'.[8]

The philosophers' judgement proved correct. The delegates on the Human Rights Commission had remarkably few disagreements over which principles should be included in the Declaration.[9] (Their disputes were chiefly political, arising out of the antagonistic relations between the Soviet Union and the United States.) On 10 December 1948, the document was adopted by the UN General Assembly as a 'common standard of achievement'.

---

5   Ibid.
6   Jacques Maritain, 'Introduction', Ibid., p. 9.
7   Ibid., p. 10.
8   Ibid.
9   For a detailed account, see Mary Ann Glendon, *A World Made New: Eleanor Roosevelt and the Universal Declaration of Human Rights*, Random House, New York, 2001.

Against the predictions of sceptics, the non-binding Declaration quickly showed its moral force. It became the principal inspiration of the post-war international human rights movement; the most influential model for the majority of rights instruments in today's world; and it continues to serve as the single most important reference point for discussions of human rights in international settings. It is a classic example of the effectiveness of what Matláry and others call 'soft power'.

Still, the decision to proceed 'without asking why' had costs, as one of the UNESCO philosophers foresaw it would. In a prescient essay titled, 'The Philosophic Bases and Material Circumstances of the Rights of Man', Richard McKeon warned that so long as the business of foundations remained unfinished, the Declaration would be highly vulnerable to struggles for the control of its interpretation 'for the purpose of advancing special interests'.[10] That is precisely what happened all during the Cold War, and in the culture battles that succeeded it, such as those at recent UN conferences where Matláry had the opportunity to see the new 'norm entrepreneurs' in action. But Mrs Roosevelt's Commission was under such pressure to proceed, and the philosophers were so confident that foundations could be found, that they left the job of proving it for another day.

Now that day has come. In Europe, with a vast supranational experiment under way, the problem has acquired increasing urgency. As Matláry puts it, 'the move toward a state based on human rights, away from the "one-nation, one-identity" state happens while there is less and less belief in the ability to define these rights in an objective manner' (p. 12).

What needs to be investigated is not whether agreement can be reached on a single foundation. Maritain and his

---

[10] Richard McKeon, 'The Philosophic Bases and Material Circumstances of the Rights of Man', in *Human Rights: Comments and Interpretations*, Wingate, London, 1949, pp. 35–6.

colleagues considered that to be a fruitless endeavour. More promising, they thought, was to demonstrate that human rights could be firmly grounded in the world's major cultural, philosophical and religious traditions. John Paul II concurred in their view, writing that, 'It is thus the task of the various schools of thought – in particular the communities of believers – to provide the moral bases for the juridical edifice of human rights.'[11]

Friends of human rights should be grateful, therefore, to Janne Haaland Matláry for taking up that challenge with spirit and energy. In this collection of essays, she makes a strong case that foundations for human rights can be found through human reason, specifically, through retrieving and reanimating the classical tradition of rationalism that was once the pride of western civilization. Like John Paul II, Benedict XVI, and other thinkers in that tradition, she also insists that reflection on human rights must begin with an adequate understanding of the human person. She thus builds her analysis of politics with far more promising materials than the instrumental rationality and the radically individualistic concept of the person that have prevented the human rights movement thus far from reaching its full potential.

Professor Mary Ann Glendon
Harvard Law School

---

[11] John Paul II, 'Address to the Diplomatic Corps Accredited to the Holy See', 9 January 1989, par. 7.

INTRODUCTION

This book is controversial, but ought not to be. It argues that a profound relativism in Europe leads to political processes that seek to redefine fundamental human rights. But human rights ought not to be redefined. The attempt to do so is the issue that should be controversial.

Europe has become the major exponent of human rights, democracy, and the rule of law all over the world. This modern 'trinity' of values has become the universal standard for good government and humane politics. While democracy entails a basic equality as the main norm, it is in human rights that we today find the values about the human being expressed in the form of so-called fundamental human rights. Rule of law means that there is a separation of powers with an independent judiciary. There can be no real democracy and rule of law unless it is based on human rights.

No one today questions the legitimacy of human rights as the basis for democracy; the procedure whereby the people decide. Rule of law reflects the same human rights, and constrains the majority when it deviates from these standards. Human rights hang logically together with democracy and rule of law: these legal and political institutions cannot exist without the assumption of a certain and very specific view of the human person – anthropology. Conversely, human rights require democracy and rule of law – these rights are not respected under tyranny, oligarchy or any kind of one-party system.

Human rights have become the new political 'Bible' in two ways – as the only point of reference in a relativist political community – but also as the source of legitimacy in political debates: no actor can 'afford' to be seen to violate human rights. It is extremely important to be in accordance with human rights in modern European politics; they thus carry a great deal of power in themselves. Yet there is often a denial that they can be objectively defined, something which undermines the authority of these rights in the long run.

There are thus at least *two paradoxes* at work here: while Europe and the West extol the rest of the world to follow human rights and in fact use this as conditions for aid and cooperation, European politicians simultaneously refuse to define, in an objective manner, what these rights really mean. Secondly, while these rights are appealed to more and more, they are undermined as sources of authority in the erosion of the belief that they can be defined in a clear and objective way.

In her analysis *Rights Talk* from 1991, Harvard law professor Mary Ann Glendon writes: 'Discourse about rights has become the principal language that we use in public settings to discuss weighty questions of right and wrong, but time and again it proves inadequate, or leads to a standoff of one right against another. The problem is not, however, as some contend, with the very notion of rights, or with our strong rights tradition. It is with a new version of rights discourse that has achieved dominance over the last thirty years.'[1] This new rights discourse is characterized, says Glendon, by the proclamation of ever new rights that are the properties of 'the lone-rights bearer' as she aptly calls him, one who has no duties and who pursues his own interests in the form of new rights: 'As various new rights are proclaimed and proposed, the catalog of individual liberties expands without much consideration of the ends to which they are oriented, their

---

[1]   M. A. Glendon, *Rights Talk: The Impoverishment of Political Discourse*, p. x.

relationship to one another, to corresponding responsi-
bilites, or to the general welfare.'[2] These two processes are
intertwined, and are symptoms of a deeper crisis in
European politics: that of an ever greater irrationality and
relativism. This is the theme of this book.

Human rights were codified as a response to the political and legal relativism of Hitler's Germany and the
Second World War, which put in a nutshell the relativist
problem of obeying orders from the legal ruler of the
realm – in this case Hitler – when these orders were
contrary to morality. The Nuremburg trials laid down that
it is wrong to obey such orders; that there is in fact a
'higher law' – a natural law if you will – that not only
forbids compliance, but which also makes it a crime to
follow such orders. In the wake of this revolutionary
conclusion in international affairs – it was the first time in
history where a court had adjudicated in such a way –
there was a growing movement to specify what this
'natural law' for the human being entailed. This resulted
in the Universal Declaration of Human Rights only three
years later – as we shall see, a supra-national set of inherent and inalienable rights for every human being. It is very
clear that the statement of human rights was to be a
'common standard for all mankind', as stated in the
preamble, and not something that could be changed at will
by political actors. Yet this is exactly what happens in
Europe today.

We would seem to have come a long way after the
Second World War, where the Nuremburg trials instituted
human dignity as the supreme value above politics and
law by determining that orders that are unjust and violate
fundamental human dignity are to be disobeyed. As
stated, those that followed orders to exterminate Jews
were not only wrong to do so, they committed a crime
against humanity and some were punished by death. This
placing of human rights *above* national law and politics is
of extreme importance in international politics. For the

2   Ibid., p. xi.

first time a tribunal judged according to the natural law of what a human being can demand and expect. The Universal Declaration of Human Rights in 1948 is the authoritative document in the world on this topic.

The rights defined in this document are parts of a whole, making up a fullness of rights which reflect a very specific anthropology. The rights are clear and concise, and the underlying anthropology is equally clear. The intention of the authors of the declaration was to put into a solemn document the insight about human dignity that could be gleaned from an honest examination, through reason and experience, of what the human being is. Therefore they wrote explicitly that 'these rights are inviolable and *inherent*. In other words, these rights could not be changed* by politicians or others, because they were inborn, belonging to every human being as a birthright, by virtue of being a human being. The declaration is a natural law document which was put into paragraphs by representatives from all over the world, from all regions and religions. Human rights are *pre-political* in the sense that they are not given or granted by any politicians to their citizens, but are 'discovered' through human reasoning as being constitutive of the human being itself. They are also therefore *apolitical* because they are not political constructs, but anthropological – consequences of our human nature. As one of the key drafters of the declaration, Charles Malik, said: 'When we disagree about what human rights mean, we disagree about what human nature is.' The very concept of human rights is therefore only meaningful if we agree that there is one common human nature which can be known through the discovery of reason.

This last statement is however at great odds with contemporary mentality, which is relativist and subjectivist, scorning the idea that human nature as such exists and even more so that it can be known through reason. But if this is denied, and we regard human rights as something that mere political processes can change, how can we uphold human rights as a standard for others, if not for ourselves? European foreign policy today is firmly based on human rights observation in all regions of the world, and entry into organizations such as the EU or NATO, the Organization for Security and Cooperation in Europe (OSCE) or the Council of Europe (COE) – the four major ones in Europe – are based on meeting human rights standards (Matláry, 2002). Thus, to know what human rights objectively mean is more than a matter for the philosophically inclined.

But even more important is European politics itself: we are moving away from the nation-state based on 'nation', one common ethnic, religious, and cultural identity in a country; towards a European polity based on human rights. We are developing several identities in the postmodern period, and the traditional state based on the forging of one 'nation' – Frenchmen, Englishmen, Spaniards – will disappear. Instead we live in multi-ethnic, multi-religious, and above all, secular, society. Our only basis for common values resides in the concept of human rights. If these cannot be defined in a clear manner, we are in a state of ethical anarchy.

A further very important issue is that we are undermining the very concept of human rights through 'politicizing' it at both the national and the international level. There is a ferocious and continuous process of redefining individual human rights in areas of contention, such as the family, children's rights, women's rights, and so on. The many UN conferences in the 1990s were arenas for such redefinition, and at national level in Europe now we see that this activity has centre stage. But when, for example, marriage and family are redefined in national laws, this seems to be a contravention of the supranational human rights standards. Again, since human rights are 'above' politics, they are also above the nation-state. They are truly supra-national; many of them also so in a legally binding form, as treaties and conventions. Each time national politics makes its own definition of a human right, it not only redefines it, but also flouts its international commitment. This in turn undermines the whole human rights edifice. This is truly a paradox for those states which uphold the 'sanctity' of human rights to other states; often rogue or failed states. They in turn can say: 'If European states can define human rights at will, why can't we?'

Thus, in the period after the founding of the UN and the development of human rights, European states have become the foremost proponents of human rights worldwide, along with the USA. By now compliance with human rights, democracy and rule of law are the standard criteria for foreign aid, cooperation, admission to international organizations, and general respect as a member of the international community. 'Human rights conditionality', which includes the criteria of democracy and rule of law, are indeed the key characteristics of the foreign policy of the EU, the OSCE, and the Council of Europe as well as individual European states. We should therefore expect that European states are model democracies, ready to teach others from their experience. We should expect that there is a clear value basis – that of universal human rights – in these states, and that voters as well as politicians should be very clear about the objective definition of these rights. Indeed, without the values embedded in human rights as the platform, there can be no rule of law or democratic system. It is human rights that form the very basis for these institutions.

But in Europe today the reality is very different. There is no clear basis of human rights, but an intense struggle over the interpretation of these rights, and often a major discrepancy between what a state proclaims in solemn international conferences and domestic policy. The EU constitutional treaty has left out the key terms 'inherent' and 'inalienable' in the bill of rights, and has failed to retain the language on heterosexual marriage and family.

In more general terms, while 'the right to life' is the first and primary human right according to the Universal Declaration, most European states have had abortion on the law books for many decades. While the right to marry is defined as a right for 'every man and woman' in the same declaration, same-sex 'marriage' is increasingly introduced in European states. While children have a right to know and be raised by their biological parents or in a similar situation according to the *Convention on the Rights of the Child* (1989), this seems to be ignored when children are 'produced' from anonymous donors. While the family is firmly defined as the basic and natural cell of society in the declaration, it is redefined by many nation states and often the state does not have policies that support the family. While the right to special societal protection for mother and child is defined in the declaration, motherhood is often regarded as a drawback for women in the European labour market, and mothers are discriminated against. While the family has a right to a sustainable income, and a just wage, in the declaration, labour rights are more and more neglected in European states and individual taxation makes a mockery of the concept of 'family income'. While religious freedom includes the right to public and private worship, Muslims are met with suspicion and opposition when they want to erect a mosque, and other religions, including the predominant one in Europe, Christianity, are pushed back into the private sphere.

As stated, there is a curious situation; a *paradox*, in the many discrepancies between the human rights professed, especially abroad, and the political reality at home in Europe.

But the paradox is even more glaring when we consider the trend towards *not* defining the values underlying European democracy. By this I mean the trend towards complete subjectivism, even nihilism: you have your opinion; I have mine; and those that say that there are objective definitions of norms – *Grundbegriffe* – are fundamentalist and undemocratic. This trend is extremely dangerous, as this kind of subjectivism undermines democracy and paves the way for totalitarianism: might then eventually becomes right when there is no standard by which to determine right. The old ideological differences have mostly gone since the Cold War, and have not been replaced. Instead, individual preferences dominate politics.

Examples of this often well-intended subjectivism abound: some time ago Norwegian papers reported that an Islamic website in Oslo argued for polygamy, which is forbidden in Norway. The religious congregation behind this website received state subsidies, as do most churches as well, from the Norwegian state. But instead of condemning polygamy and withdrawing the subsidy, the minister of culture stated that 'in a democracy we have freedom of expression'.[3] What ought she to have done? Polygamy contradicts the human right to marry as defined in the Universal Declaration of Human Rights. In addition, Norway has had a Christian culture for more than a thousand years and is still a majority Christian culture. Thus, it ought to be easy to reject polygamy. But why are we so unsure about what is right and what is wrong, what is condemnable and what is not?

There are several issues here: on the one hand, we see a degree of secularization in Europe whereby people no longer know their Christian roots and therefore do not know which values Christianity has contributed to politics and law. They are therefore unsure of the relationship between their own 'majority culture' and human rights. This happens while large numbers of immigrants arrive in Europe from other cultures and with other religions. There is a basic insecurity about what to think of cases like the above: what is intolerant, what is religiously founded and protected by religious freedom, etc. This is such an acute problem because the move towards a state based on human rights, away from the 'one nation, one identity' state, happens while there is less and less belief in the ability to define these rights in an objective manner. The anthropological crisis, so to speak, coincides with the greatest transformation of the European state since its inception at Westphalia in 1648. We are at the same time transforming the legitimacy basis of the state to human rights while claiming that these human rights cannot be

---

[3]   *Aftenposten*, 12.1.2004, front page.

defined objectively. This is a dangerous situation where 'normative anarchy' threatens. It is obvious that no state can exist without a set of common values held by all citizens. Today, lacking a common Christian identity and increasingly lacking the firm grip of national identity, we have embraced the human rights identity – we profess human rights as our only value basis, so to speak, as the only possible modern ideology. But if we refuse the possibility of defining these rights, what is left but normative anarchy?

The trend towards nihilism, a hundred years after Friedrich Nietzsche wrote *Beyond Good and Evil*,[4] aptly sub-titled 'Precursor to a philosophy for the future', is manifested in the lack of belief in human ability, through reasoned debate and thinking, to arrive at objective truth about human nature and human virtue and vice. This stance is pronounced and implicit in European politics today. The very concept of truth itself is not only contested, as it has always been, but seen as fundamentalist and repressive; as something undemocratic.

This strange aversion to the concept of truth is intimately linked to the concept of 'political correctness' (PC). It is perhaps the most powerful concept we have in our modern Western democracies, and is a wholly immaterial one. The power of being PC or not has been felt by most people: one senses that something which used to be *comme il faut*, suddenly is not. The media no doubt play a key role in this process of 'shaming' and 'praising'. To think that one can discover objectively valid moral truths is certainly the most 'un-PC' position possible. It is however the position argued for in this book.

The strength of PC derives precisely from the lack of belief in the result of rational debate, viz. firm and convincing conclusions. If debate is not aimed at the discovery of truth as a possibility and goal, then there is no

---

4   *Jenseits von Gut und Böse: Vorspiel einer Philosophie der Zukunft*, Wilhelm Goldmann Verlag, Munich, 1885.

point in the debate other than propaganda for own interests and values. PC today is very much about tolerance, but tolerance is an empty concept unless there is a standard for judging what is to be tolerated and what not. Should polygamy be tolerated, even if I do not like it? Clearly the minister of culture was unsure of this. Being herself a Christian Democrat, perhaps she thought that it would be very un-PC for someone profiled as a Christian to be critical of Muslims. This is the kind of dynamism I am concerned about: the lack of standard for judgement makes tolerance a PC concept in the end: one tolerates what the majority likes or that which is promoted by strong interest groups, as one is afraid of being charged with intolerance. But one only tolerates what PC condones, because PC has the power to marginalize effectively.

This subjective, media-driven power of PC is only possible because there is no search for truth, as that is assumed away as impossible and probably as basically undesirable. But with such a premise, *human rights can never exist, for they cannot be defined.* The paradox of modern European democracy is exactly this: we profess and impose human rights all over the globe, but refuse to define the substance of these rights at home. We hold that they mean what we choose them to mean at any one time; thereby making PC the guiding star of politics. The majority of voters do not speak out in referenda on these issues, but so-called 'public opinion' is moulded in media-driven campaigns, often in clever alliances with single-interest groups. Part of this 'norm entrepreneurship' is to 'shame' and intimidate minority views and to create an appearance of majority opinion through clever uses of the media. Thus, in this way the 'tolerance' claimed becomes deeply intolerant. The end result is that might becomes right, the logical implication of extreme subjectivism.

This book is about symptoms, diagnosis, and a possible cure. The symptoms here refer to the paradox of human rights and European democracy: on the one hand, human rights reign supreme as our 'export article' and bequest to the world; on the other hand, we refuse to define these rights as universally valid, constant, even eternal, human rights. We no longer believe that there is a human nature and therefore human rights, and we no longer believe that the concept of truth is meaningful. But how can we avoid turning democracy into tyranny under these conditions?

I try to diagnose the problem in Part One of the book. The intention is to unearth the underlying values of our societies in Europe. Depressingly, they centre on materialism in both a consumerist and anthropological sense. In terms of what we assume and believe, the picture is one of a strangely pervasive subjectivism: nothing seems to be considered universally valid, there is no common basic structure: *Grundbegriffe*, as the Germans say more precisely. The spiritual search that we see many manifestations of, takes on forms that border on the superstitious and escapist; from New Age to 'religion à la carte'. The political search for ideology becomes one of fashionable personalities and cheap sound-bites rather than serious politicians who talk about issues in their complexity. Some call this picture one of postmodernism. I think this is misleading. We are not in a situation of going beyond modernity in the sense of the historical modern period in Europe, but in a period where the transmitted moral codes and the standard ways of rational reasoning are scrapped at the same time. But democracy and law both presuppose reason and a certain set of values: equality before the law ultimately implies an anthropology, in fact that human nature can be defined and is the very same across time and cultures.

In *Chapter One* I present the anthropological point of departure for contemporary European politics, contrasting it with the classical ideal of 'political man'. I want to underline that democracy in its classical form was premised on a specific anthropology – that man is able to become truly human, through the search for the common good of the *polis* sphere. Politics was the highest form of human activity after philosophy, which deals with the soul. But what happens to democracy when there is no civic sense, no ideology; only self-interest in a material sense, as is prevalent in Europe today? If 'self-referential man' is typical of European anthropology today, how can human rights become anything but 'read me my rights'-thinking? It is a disturbing feature of modern European politics that one invokes the human rights language to reach any political goal one favours, without regard for the underlying logic of these same human rights. One hears arguments that are logically mutually exclusive – such as saying that there is no contradiction between the family definition of the Universal Declaration and the 'homosexual family', but just an extension of 'the family' to 'many types of families' – as if logic as we know it no longer plays any role. This may be because the logical sense is completely lost, but also because the term 'human rights' simply has become the most effective slogan for advancing any cause in the political debate. When one's only reference point is oneself and one's own preferences, then human rights cannot be anything but a political process, ever changing.

In *Chapter Two* the broader question of European democracy is posed: how does it function when based on 'self-referential man' as opposed to the classical dictum of public virtue, of seeking the common good? Here I try to show how far European democracy has deviated from the classical democratic norm. The point is not to deny the major differences that must exist between this ideal and any reality, but to ask whether we can sustain a democracy when there is no public virtue involved: when 'private interests' become the only political reference points. The problem today is the lack of common principles and values; 'common standards' as the human rights declaration puts it. We simultaneously reject the moral standards of Christianity and embrace private, subjective moral standards. I argue that the lack of moral standards, 'common values', is the Achilles heel of contemporary European democracy.

In *Chapter Three* I present an analysis of the fundamental human rights of the international rights instruments, first and foremost the Universal Declaration. I am especially concerned with the underlying anthropology of these rights, and with the way in which the rights were arrived at. This was a process of reasoned discovery; not a political process of bargaining, although the people that drafted the declaration had to steer clear of many political obstacles.

Moral nihilism meets human rights: as stated, European states are now leaving the period of the 'nation-state' based on one national identity, becoming pluralistic states through integration and immigration, globalization and not least, through the postmodern outlook on life. This chapter focuses on the implications of a moral relativism married to human rights as the basis of society. What will self-referential man do when his only 'values' are human rights, but when these rights are defined at will? We look at the example of religious freedom in this chapter: on how this human rights now replaces the principle of a national religion; often termed the principle of *cuius regio, eius religio*, which means that the ruler of a state chooses the religion of his subjects. This principle, laid down in the treaties of Westphalia in 1648, became the basis for 'state churches' in Europe. Now European states can no longer claim this in the face of article 18 of the Universal Declaration of Human Rights, on religious freedom. But if the European state is to successfully transform itself to a human rights-based community, then the inhabitants must know what the much contested and very controversial article 18 really means in objective terms. The need for definition is obvious, and will be so for other human rights as well, the more the European state relies on this source of common values. This chapter also seeks to determine how far Europe has embraced human rights in this regard, by analysis of the European Convention on Human Rights and the new EU constitution, which are both legally and supra-nationally binding.

Chapter Four deals with the growing importance of human rights in global business life.

Part Two of this book deals with how the redefinition of

human rights is sought, both at the national and the international level.

In *Chapter Five* I contrast the natural law process of human rights reasoning – the one argued for in this book – with the contemporary political process of human rights redefinition. Here I look at how 'norm entrepreneurs' seek to change human rights, and why human rights 'language' is so vital in the form of so-called 'soft law' in UN conferences especially. There is a new and rapidly growing body of international texts that come out of international conferences, especially at the UN, and these texts, although not legally binding as international law, are nonetheless of major political importance. They form, so to speak, the emerging international consensus on an issue, and many argue that human rights evolve and are expanding in this manner. From a relativist point of view this is certainly entirely logical – if there is no human nature that is fixed, and therefore no fixed human rights, then human rights are what we determine them to be at any one time, through a political process. The underlying philosophical premises are never made explicit, but the political process is very evident and very important. Once a textual reference to a 'new' human right has been achieved, this has authority at home in national politics because the UN, the concept of human rights, etc. in and of themselves carry legitimacy. The 'norm entrepreneurs' then import the new 'right' and demand national compliance with this.

This view of seeing human rights is at the very core of the problem: how can they be standards against which to measure compliance and non-compliance, violations and state action, if they are ever-changing? Yet there is no doubt that this way of seeing human rights is the prevalent one today. This is because ethical or moral questions are regarded as essentially to be determined by majority voting or at least by public opinion. In national politics in Scandinavia, the concept of the 'consensus conference' has been introduced as a way of resolving difficult issues. If a consensus among experts and interested parties can be had, then we resolve the issue in this way.

In *Chapter Six* I analyse how human rights are internationalized and supra-nationalized, in terms of Europe in particular. But at the same time politics is more and more 'legalized', while human rights are interpreted by judges who increasingly feel that they play with politics. The quest for the *Rechtsstaat* is therefore now one of international and not national politics, and a very difficult one at that.

Chapter Seven analyses cases where the redefinition of human rights is sought: the family, and religious freedom. Here I contrast the actual definition of these rights in human rights instruments with both ongoing political processes in Europe and in the UN setting, and their interaction. The major point is to bring out which type of political *reasoning* is acceptable and legitimate in these processes. As we will see, this is the reasoning based on the concept of 'self-referential' man. There is no reasoning from a principled analysis of human nature and from the other human rights; but a selective concentration on only one aspect of human rights – or on one right only – and a strategic use of the human rights label to promote a single type of interest. Human rights become instrumentalized when 'used' like this.

To sum up, the diagnosis presented in Part One and Part Two of the book concludes that the major problem with European democracy today is its lack of a common normative framework for political action. This is most obvious in human rights politics – while Europe is basing its democracy increasingly on human rights, its politicians are less and less willing to accept that this must and does imply a specific set of moral principles derived from a specific anthropology, or human nature. 'Self-referential' man will not do.

But how can this anthropology be rediscovered? How can we again learn to reason properly and correctly about politics? Is there a way to discover common principles? This is the subject of Part Three of this book. It seeks to 'resurrect' the classical tradition of rationalism; of natural law thinking and reasoning. If we accept that there is a need for objective standards for any democracy – as made evident in the analysis of human rights – then we must ask how to proceed in order to arrive at these.

Thankfully Europe contains the answer to this. Whereas both the concepts of human rights and democracy originated in Europe, they did so in a philosophical and religious context of natural law reasoning.

Natural law is simple: it is about the human ability to discern – *ratio* – right from wrong, good from bad. These terms are not about the 'self-referential' in man; they are on the contrary necessarily about the universals – about what is valid for me and you and everyone, about human nature as such. I argue that political and legal reasoning necessarily must concern universals, i.e. the common good. It cannot be 'self-referential', because then it is not about law or politics. If I say that the law should punish stealing, it is because I argue that stealing as such is wrong, and therefore should be punished. It is about a universal, and the law condemns it as a universal. But if I say that it is wrong to have a boat for sailing and that having one should be condemned, I am speaking nonsense. It simply does not make sense. This is because there is nothing universally valid about having a boat. The language we use indicates to us immediately that we speak about universals in the first case, of law and politics; but only about particulars, i.e. about the boat as a private pursuit, in the second instance. This Aristotelian language is as relevant today as it was in his time, for it shows the way to the distinction between private and political, between morally relevant and irrelevant.

Res publica – the 'political thing' – was the polity itself, the republic or the state, as a modern rendering would translate it. The political is that which concerns the *polis*, human society. To the ancient Greek masters of political thought, political activity was the most important and noble human activity after philosophy, which crowned human endeavour because it concerned the very soul of man itself.

The reason why politics is key to human happiness and subsistence is anthropological: it is because the human being is a *zoon politikon*, a political being, a social being. Man naturally lives in society, is naturally social – in the family, but also beyond it. He is also naturally *rational*; indeed, the rational ability distinguishes him from animals, according to Plato, Aristotle, and later Thomas Aquinas and the mainstream of our European political philosophy. Because any man can reason about basic facts, including basic facts about right and wrong, he is different from animals, who also have language, but who cannot reason. This observation is the basis for the natural law tradition which has formed European democracy.

As Aristotle and Plato pointed out, man has an ability for creating good or bad societies. The human propensity for evil lies at the root of tyranny, while the best and most virtuous thought results in what they termed aristocracy. While we prefer democracy to aristocracy today as the form of government, it is important to realize at the outset that human nature and the quality of society hang together: it can go both ways – we can have bad societies or good ones. The science of politics, founded by these ancient thinkers, was both normative and empirical: the question they asked was this: What is the best society? Then they analysed various types of societies that they observed – Aristotle inductively and empirically, comparing known city-states; Plato deductively, through the reasoning of Socrates. Both were however informed by the over-arching question: what is *good* society? Which is the *best* society?

The point here is simply that anthropology and politics are connected: society is a reflection of the 'goodness' or 'badness' of its inhabitants, or to put it in more traditional terms, it is a function of virtue and vice. In a democracy the voters are themselves the decision-makers; thus it is incumbent on them to be virtuous. In a monarchy, aristocracy, oligarchy or tyranny – ancient forms of the polity – the key to society was the virtue or vice of a few persons. A good monarchy could decline into a tyranny, and a good aristocracy could decline into an oligarchy, which was morally speaking a bad form of government.

Today this rather obvious and also substantial link between the moral qualities of the decision-makers and the ensuing political society is not much reflected on. To say that politics is about moral issues seems strange, as one would rather be inclined to agree that politics is amoral or even immoral. But even when people say that 'Politics is a dirty business', they are in fact affirming that it is supposed to be something very different: they mean that it is wrong that politics is not better, more morally sound, when they say this with regret and disdain. They are not describing what politics is per se, like money laundering or murder. They do not mean that politics is defined as a 'dirty business' as such, but that a particular political society they happen to know, is 'dirty'.

But where do we find the natural law tradition that we need so much in European democracy today? The answer to this is startling to many and politically incorrect to even more. We find this tradition at its richest and most modern development, in an 'up-dated' version, so to speak, in the Catholic Church. It is church tradition and church thinkers that have continued to develop natural law and apply it to modern politics and democracy, and it is only here that we today can find such contemporary analyses. This body of political reasoning is often termed 'the social teaching' natural law thinking as well as present-day analysis. There is in fact a fully-fledged ideology which is based on the ancient concepts of the common good and justice, and which claims that these key concepts have precise meanings which can be arrived at through human reasoning.

But the major contributor to this analysis is not ancient, but very contemporary. *Chapter Seven* discusses the relationship between natural law and Christianity, and in *Chapter Eight* I present the centrality of human rights to the papal 'politics' of the late Pope John Paul II. His papacy was one of human rights; he was always concentrating on the concept of human dignity, in writing, words, and action. In *Chapter Nine* I show what Josef Ratzinger's analysis of relativism and democracy amounts to: a clear restatement of the *Grundbegriffe*, the anthropology that was diagnosed as the problem of European democracy at the outset of this book. The political manipulation of human rights comes about because modern man lacks the ability to reason clearly about man in society, about 'political man', and first of all, to know what this man is, as a human being.

This book is about the connection between rationalism and democracy; about the need for objective standards of truth and logic that is implicit in the very concept of human rights which constitutes the 'ideology' of modern democracy. It is neither about ancient thinkers or ancient societies, nor about political philosophy or utopias, but about contemporary European democracy. There is a paradox today in how citizens talk more and more about human rights, about freedom, and about finding one's own identity, while one is unwilling to consider the anthropological question, viz. what a human being is. Human nature, its greatness and vileness, was a common reference point for all philosophy, also political philosophy, for several millennia. Now the transmission of this knowledge and the belief that there is a human nature is curiously absent. Tolerance seems to be the only democratic 'value' in our societies, but it is a term that cannot be defined as long as we have no standard for saying what is tolerable and what is intolerable. The lack of a reference point for what is right and wrong represents the gravest danger to a democracy simply because one cannot say which values this kind of society should promote and aim at. The relativist assumption, which is so dominant today, is at the core of the current crisis because it cannot co-exist with democracy.

This may seem startling, even absurd: isn't democracy about unlimited freedom and pluralism, about free choice, without authority? Isn't it the final liberation from imposition? The answer is yes and no; yes in most things political, where there are many options to choose from; but no in the sphere of fundamental virtues and vices. If one is a moral relativist, one would have to agree with

Douglas and not Lincoln that slavery is OK when a majority votes in favour of it, or that Hitler must be allowed to rule since he was democratically elected. In our own day we would have to agree that not only is abortion and euthanasia acceptable as long as the majority wants to legislate in favour; we would also have to accept ethnic cleansing or genocide in the same manner. Most people however would object to at least some of these propositions – I would guess that most would say that ethnic cleansing and genocide are evil, and also that Hitler was a tyrant who should be deposed.

There is something very illogical here: on the one hand we have a 'feeling' of right and wrong, but we think that it is a mere feeling because we lack the ability to justify or explain why we 'feel' like this. We do not know how to reason about these matters. On the other hand we are uncomfortable with the proposition that there can be moral laws underlying politics and that democracy is intended to promote good morals in society, that it is fundamentally about values, not about procedures. We would like to say something like this: 'Morals belong to one's private life and have nothing to do with the freedom of democracy, which is about following rules and accepting difference.'

For many centuries European democracies have shared approximately the same moral norms, derived from the ancient and Christian legacy. The Ten Commandments were more or less acceptable to all. These moral rules were also reflected in law and politics. There was no essential contestation of what should be taught in school or punished in the criminal code. The family was a given and natural institution; the right to life was not an issue in politics, and there was a basic agreement on what belonged to the private and the public sphere. True, different political ideologies had different views on the latter, and also on the role of the family in the economic and societal structure, but these were debates about the role of the state, of the relationship between economics and politics, and when it came down to the anthropological issues, it was a debate over the existence of the soul – of whether man was simply material or not.

Today there is no overt, systemic ideological debate. The political is fragmented and un-ideological because the discussion is no longer about man and society, about what the good society is, based on what man is. It is rather the situation that Friedrich Nietzsche diagnosed over a century ago in his book *Beyond Good and Evil*.

PART ONE

HUMAN RIGHTS:
THE POLITICAL 'BIBLE'

CHAPTER ONE

'JENSEITS VON GUT UND BÖSE'? SELF-REFERENTIAL MAN[1]

We seem to live in happy times in Europe. We have material prosperity, unparalleled in history. We live longer and control our lives more than any time before. We seem to be the true masters of our own destiny. We are better educated than any generation before us, and technology and medicine have progressed to an astonishing degree. Illiteracy has been abolished, and everyone has been through a general education. University is within the reach of almost everyone, and women for the first time play their rightful role in society, in all professions and in politics.

From the post-Second World War generation until today there seems to have been a steady line of progress. We have undone the tyrants. We have democracy in all Western states. We can decide ourselves on our social, economic, and political fate.

We ought to live in the best of all worlds, as Rousseau would have put it. There are no authorities that decide for us; indeed, no authority is recognized by most people.

Freedom is the word that comes to mind. The freedom

---

[1] Part of this chapter is based on my book *Faith through Reason*, German edition *Love-Story: So wurde ich katolisch*, St Ulrich Verlag, Augsburg, 2004.

we enjoy is unparalleled: traditional expectations of how we should live have disappeared. In fact, nothing handed down by tradition has any authority over us. This is seen as great progress by most people.

What characterizes our time? How is it different from earlier times? Is it better now than before? There is of course no definite answer to the last question, but I think that we can safely say that there is a discrepancy between our material progress, which is undisputable, and the realization of the good society, which is somehow unrelated to things. The Europe of today is one of consumerism and individualism, and the citizen seems less and less able to determine his own fate and that of society. Market forces play ever greater roles and the citizen turns into consumer. But there is less and less knowledge of the political; what it means to be a citizen. The European person has become an expert consumer, but an ignorant and indifferent citizen. This is not a development wrought by design, but a consequence of many factors. In this book I argue that the main problem lies at the level of human choice, of the choice for maximum freedom and individualism, as opposed to the possible choice of the classical notion of politics as the 'common good'. Yet even more basic than this individual choice are the assumptions about human nature that condition them; the primary one here is the assumption that there is no human nature. There are therefore no moral axioms to be discovered, and law is not guided bythen.

The prevalent anthropology or view of man is materialist in the sense of consumption; but there is also a thorough materialism about life itself. Old ties of community and family erode, and the single person lives basically for himself. One can have an entirely *autistic* life in society, living for oneself only, in one's own universe. The centre of life, its very meaning seems to be me, my own person. I must be successful, happy, satisfied; protect myself against sickness, old age and most of all, death. And there are no obvious tasks – society and family do not need me. This is especially pronounced for young people.

Our time – my time, the time of the post-war period, of the generation of the 60s and 70s – is marked by three features: *materialism, subjectivism,* and *utilitarianism.*
Materialism is both about having and buying, about consuming. But it is also about seeing persons as mere objects, as things. *Subjectivism* is about seeing everything in relation to the own self; deciding that nothing exists outside the self, and that no norms of right and wrong exist in themselves. My opinion about these matters is all there can be. *Utilitarianism* is about using others to our own advantage; we calculate about people: are they useful to us?

These features are much more evident today than in my parents' generation, during the war. We seek meaning in ourselves, in our self-fulfilment. Everything revolves around the self.

Materialism

Materialism is no newcomer to the West. It has always been a steady incentive for human activity, and as such, is useful. But today the pressure of consuming and buying seems to be much stronger than ever before. The market logic of buying and selling is everywhere, penetrating virtually all spheres of society. My children are bombarded by advertisements, and constantly crave new things and new clothes. It is also much easier to acquire these things, which has the effect that they lose their value to us. We simply don't appreciate things that are too easily acquired.

Material progress has been a prime goal in our lives in the entire post-war period. When I was little, I remember how my mother – and the other housewives in the neighbourhood – discussed what new furniture they could buy that year, which new car, which new clothes, and so on. Status was measured in these showpieces of progress. Norwegian society, my own, was very egalitarian, but this also meant that all families could acquire more or less the same things. This was tangible progress in the post-war era, modelled on the dream of American consumerism. All families could gradually build their own home, get their own car, aspire to a weekend home, then get a little boat, and so on.

But the post-war reconstruction was also a *common* nation-building project, and as such had a social and political side. It was consumption with an end, viz. that of rebuilding a society. Consumption today is excessive by comparison: it is a consumption mostly built on created needs, which is endlessly being renewed because the market profits from it. The common man and woman today are largely prisoners of market forces. They are tempted to want ever new things, new luxuries. Life is more and more concentrated on acquiring these things. There is no critical distance to the market, which dominates society and our lives far too much. This kind of materialism makes us appreciate appearances: Do I look rich? Do I have the social status that others admire? Am I on a par with my fellows in terms of possessions? Do I feel materially 'on top'?

The less we are mature as human beings, the easier we fall prey to materialism. The things possess and dominate us, not *vice versa*. Without the things the market tells me I need, I am nothing. The market creates more than new needs; it also creates lifestyles and images, exploring the human being's search for values and meaning. The natural inclination is to ask: 'Who am I?' Today the market tells you: 'You can choose: we sell you an image which is who you are.' The young especially fall for this forgery. It goes with the idea, so common today, that there is nothing else to be found: there is no answer to the question: 'Who am I?'

There is also another kind of materialism which is closely related to the above: the view of the human person as a being made up of flesh and blood only. When the body is weak, sick, or dead, there is nothing left of the *person*.

The body *is* the human being. This materialism is as old

as history itself, but seems to me to be very prevalent in our time. It is manifested in the lack of respect for those who are physically 'sub-optimal'; but also in the idolatry of the body; in the debates over abortion and euthanasia, and in the general, but often implicit view of each other as acceptable only when we are physically strong, young, and attractive.

The 'objectification' – in German *Verdinglichung*, literally 'making into a thing' – is visible in the abortion and euthanasia debates. The unborn, the old and the sick are somehow less human than the rest of us. The fact that they are weak and sick reduces their claim to being fully human. When the body is near death, it seems that it is no longer fully entitled to equal treatment as a human being. The political debate on introducing euthanasia is only possible because we have a tremendous distance to those persons about whom we debate. We are not talking about ourselves at all, but about someone with less 'humanness' than us. The material view of the other is the reason why this is possible. It defines humanness as a function of health, age, and success – of *material* appearances.

Others that are endangered by the material view of man today are the poor, the handicapped, and the otherwise marginalized. We don't see them at all, and we secretly think that they are worth less than us because they are weaker. They call for respect, mercy, and real solidarity, but they are somehow excluded from the universe of the successful and the 'normal'.

When one reads the international human rights instruments, one encounters the phrase 'human dignity' which is the only and the very basis for human rights. What does 'dignity' mean? It is not something one can see and touch, but it is nonetheless a recognizable quality. Every person possesses dignity, says the UN's Universal Declaration of Human Rights of 1948 and all later human rights instruments.

Once when I negotiated in a UN conference for the Holy See, I had a meeting with the Norwegian delegation of the then socialist government. They were very suspicious about my insistence that women have dignity. 'What is that word "dignity", they said, some sort of bourgeois repressiveness?'

Dignity is what makes a human being a person, and it is a completely non-material quality, although the body also has dignity. You show that you recognize the other person's dignity when you respect him, but when you treat him as an object, as a thing, as material, then you deny him this dignity. To show respect is the major indication that you know what dignity is.

Utilitarianism

Our time is characterized by utilitarianism. This is the tendency to see other people as things to be used, as objects. When women are represented as sexual objects, they are used, not respected. In interpersonal relations there is a great deal of utilitarianism, viz. the confusion of a person and a thing. A person can never be possessed, but requires respect and has his or her own dignity. A person simply *is* in his uniqueness. A thing is an *object* made to serve us; while persons are never made to be used by others, but to be respected as human beings. A person should receive this respect simply by virtue of being, not by virtue of being useful.

In our time there is a very utilitarian view of people. Love is presented in media and popular culture as self-satisfaction: I love a person because he pleases my ego. He satisfies my needs. Sexuality is not about self-giving, but about acquiring sexual satisfaction. Thus it becomes a kind of self-love by extension: this or that person reinforces my ego, my view of myself. Very much what passes for love today is in reality the opposite; utility.

The same kind of utilitarianism can be seen in professional as well as private relationships. In professional life, networks are the key to success, and this is perhaps just appropriate, but when private friends become friends as a result of calculation, it is wrong. In the family we may find the only place where calculation does not enter: here people are accepted and loved as they are, organically and naturally.

In December 2001 I headed the Holy See's delegation to a UN conference on the commercial sexual exploitation of children in Japan. This kind of gruesome adult abuse of children is really the ultimate utilitarianism. We see it in sexual exploitation of women, and even of children: human beings that can be used for some perverse pleasure can be bought and sold. In such cases we can really talk about using and abusing others. The abuser is totally blind to the dignity and personality of the other human being.

We are rightly shocked by this, but we should watch our tendency to view others as objects in less blatant ways.

Self-Referential Man

Our time is also marked by an overwhelming degree of subjectivism. If I were to point to one feature of our time which is a problem from the point of view of achieving human happiness, it is precisely this subjectivism. The presumption that man can only be referring to himself in order to decide on matters in society and politics is the core problem.

By this I mean the common presumption that everything revolves around myself; that I, the ego, am the centre of the universe. Man is in many cases a prisoner of this self. This self-referential life has profound implications for politics, as is the theme of this book. If all there is in the universe is 'me', and therefore only my own subjective interests, how can politics exist? How can the term 'common good' or 'common weal' make any sense?

The pervasive contemporary subjectivism comes in many guises: one kind of subjectivism is of course plain old egoism: I want this, I desire that, I will such and such, and I do it if it pleases me. This is age-old human nature. The difference in contemporary egoism and the traditional variant seems to be that there are few, if at all any, censures against egoism today. Egoism seems OK because there are no alternatives. In previous generations one learnt that it is wrong to be egoistic, but do we learn, or even teach, the same today?

Instead we see the display of narcissism all around us: in the media, in politics, in the press: 'Look at me! I own this or that; am rich;' or: 'Look at me! I am important! I have this or that position'; or 'Look at me! I am beautiful! I look young, I am successful, I am ahead of you.' This is the message that bombards us all the time. It is not a message of admiration of good virtues – it is not a message that says 'this person is good because he has done this or that'. No, it is the constant message of a narcissistic society – of vanity and self-love.

Again, this is human nature. We are all tempted to be self-centred; in fact, we are naturally narcissistic to a great extent unless we fight consciously against it. The problem today is that we don't. But there is also the very important side to subjectivism that has to do with what the Germans call *Grundbegriffe*, or basic principles. This is a philosophical term, but one which is easy to understand: it means that there are some ordering principles or norms that come before all else and which make it possible for us to know ourselves and the world.

One such principle is for instance that human nature exists and is a universal given – all human beings share in some basic tenets of personhood.

Another is that all human beings can know certain things in life, such as basic good from basic evil. Most people still react with repulsion against evil unless they are totally corrupted, regardless of which culture or religion they belong to.

But today there is a dangerous subjectivism with regard to these *Grundbegriffe*. Some even maintain that nothing exists outside 'me', of the subject that I am. Everything is constructed in my image; nothing exists objectively, by itself, independently of me. And even if one cannot deny that a tree or a car exists objectively, one maintains that the meaning of these objects is subjective, viz. that they have a meaning for me only. Even worse: good and evil are just about personal feelings and subjective views.

Further, my version of reality is not possible to communicate to others; thus, I live in my world, you in yours, and there is no common ground between us. This is reminiscent of the invention called 'virtual reality' whereby a person lives and enters into a world of subjective experiences.

Why is this dangerous? Because it makes us inhuman and irresponsible, amoral and autistic. If my world is my private one that cannot be communicated to others, then there can be no moral norms that are objectively true. In fact, there can be no truth and no measure of truth and lie, of right and wrong. This position implies total relativism, which in turn means that politics and law rest on ever-changing subjective norms. That in turn means that eventually might becomes right and that justice cannot exist.

Traditionally we speak of ontological realism, or metaphysics, in philosophy. This refers to the position that the world – things and norms – can be known by us, and that they have an existence that is real, viz. objective. It is I, the subject that discovers these realities, through experience and deductive reasoning. But the reality of human nature and the world is a given.

Against this view there has been a long row of philosophical positions, the most famous being the struggle between the realists and the nominalists in the Middle Ages, which largely followed the split of Catholicism and Protestantism at that time. The nominalists said that there can be no knowledge of the essence of things – we know things only because we give them a name – 'nomen'. We can then change the name, and the 'thing' for which the name stood is no longer there – it does not exist apart from its name. In fact, it is only the name of a thing that we can know, not the thing or the object itself. To take a current example, the word 'family' does not stand for anything real it itself, but only for whatever we choose to call a family.

But today the old nominalism is replaced by a much more radical subjectivism which says that things are out there only to the extent that I, the subject, recognize them. They only exist in my image of them. In such a world there is nothing we can have in common – neither a belief in God, nor common ethics, nor law. The whole concept of law presupposes equality and objective treatment, and that the subjects of the law accept the law as equally valid for all. Then law must refer to universal norms – to the concept of justice as such.

Nothing is more worrisome than this constructivism in matters pertaining to the sphere of human rights and politics. For example, it is becoming commonplace to say that a family is whatever calls itself a family. Anyone living together can be a family. What is exasperating is not so much that the family concept is applied to anyone's arrangements, although this poses problems as well, but more the approach: that there is nothing to be sought that corresponds to the word 'family'. This is a radical nominalism that makes inter-subjective understanding, discussion, and decision-making ultimately impossible. If only subjective views exist, then decision-making becomes the tyranny of the majority.

The lost knowledge of human nature

If our time is characterized by these features I mention – materialism, subjectivism, and utilitarianism, was it any better before? And is there really so much wrong with this anyway? In other words, aren't I constructing a problem that is not there?

I think we are really worse off than my parents' generation because then one learnt that there are some common norms about right and wrong that are authoritative. Today there is much less agreement on this. Human nature has not changed, but the correctives to human nature have largely disappeared. Secularization accounts for much of this, as does the fragmentation of society. The sources of moral authority in society have been severely weakened, for complex reasons. These are parents, churches, and schools.

What was it our fathers knew and transmitted to us about good and bad? Perhaps they never reflected on it, but everyone 'knew' that there were rules about right and wrong, good and bad. It is bad to envy, to steal, to kill, to think only of oneself; it is good to think of others, be honest and upright, be good to others, respect them, not be overly materialistic, etc. These were the Ten Commandments transmitted as common rules of ethics. Every parent knew what these rules were, and no one really questioned them. At that time church and school transmitted the same values. There was a strong common basis of values in Western society.

This basis has eroded over the last couple of genera-tions. This has complex causes, not to be discussed here. But it remains a fact that the three institutions: parents, school, and church exert much less influence in society than before. Today there is a widespread mentality that you can live as you like; that there are no rules at all apart from the idea that tolerance is the only norm. But often this tolerance is practised quite tyrannically – only what is 'politically correct' and condoned by public opinion is tolerated. That is mostly the old liberal dictum that you can do anything as long as it does not hurt others. But today this is much more radical, for there are no norms left to restrict you.

Others' views are easily labelled 'undemocratic' and 'intolerant', especially the suggestion that there is a truth to be found and ethical norms to be discovered.

There used to be common knowledge of what are tradi-tionally known as *virtues* and *vices* in European philosophy and theology. Virtues are those qualities in a human being that make him good; vices are those that make him bad. The word 'virtue' means 'strength' – a virtuous person is a strong person. The traditional curricu-lum included reading of the classics, where philosophers like Seneca and Cicero discuss how to become a virtuous man. Plato and Aristotle, among others, also have this as the main theme in their ethical and political writings.

The human virtues include fortitude, temperance, justice, and magnanimity, to mention but a few. One should train oneself, like an athlete; become strong but just, generous and moderate. Corresponding vices include vanity, sensuality, gluttony, pride, and impatience. The goal in life is to become noble as a person, and this is done by combating the viler tendencies of human nature. Human nature was known to have both good and bad tendencies, and training was needed all the time in order to succeed in developing the virtues.

In Christianity the human virtues are developed through the specific ethics of Christ's teaching: humility as opposed to pride and vanity; charity as opposed to egoism, and so on. Christianity adds the theological virtues of faith, hope, and charity to the classical virtues.

All this knowledge of human nature and norms was handed down to us through the centuries, and somehow transmitted through the institutions I mentioned. The essential theme was to teach the human being to live a good and right life, and this could only be accomplished by a continuous struggle to become better. The term *askesis*, which we associate with a dry and inhuman life, really means to train, like an athlete.

My point here is simply that no generations before us seem to have thought that human nature is OK as it is – they have always known that it needs redemption and that to live virtuously hard work is needed. But today we don't even think that there is a universal human nature; no less that there is something useful in the traditional knowledge of virtues and vices. Speaking about virtues only makes sense when there is a common human nature anyway. And finally, even if we admit that human nature exists, there is not a conviction that virtues and vices are relevant as concepts any more.

But if you ask whether the vices are prevalent today, what you do find when you look around?

Take *gluttony*, which is the vice of over-indulging in

food and drink. Don't we see a tremendous preoccupation with food, to the point where obesity is a major problem in most Western states? Anorexia is another manifestation of this. Take *sensuality*, the vice of being overly attached to the pleasure of the senses. All around us people are valued for their looks only. What about *lust*, that very good word for excessive preoccupation with sexuality? This age is 'sexualized' to such an extent that children are deprived of the innocence of childhood by being introduced to sexuality far too early, and adults are almost 'abnormal' if they stay married to the same person for a lifetime and think that sexuality is an expression of deep commitment and love. Take *pride*, the worst vice of all. The opposite is humility, where forgetfulness of self and service to others are the signs. I do not see many humble people around. On the contrary, the ego is the centre of our attention. Take *greed*. Making money is what it's about. Getting more and more is the main goal in life for most people, it seems. Your 'market value' is the most interesting feature about you, that is, how much money you will make or how famous you are.

The 'market-value' of a prostitute is an innocent matter compared to the excessive weight put on the 'market value' of the business tycoons.

Thus, a simple rundown of the how the vices fare today gives a lot of food for thought. They seem more relevant than ever. But who today cares to ask himself: am I greedy, proud, lustful? Or am I generous, magnanimous, charitable, humble?

This has direct and grave consequences for societal and political life. The 'common good' which is what politics should be about, is a completely antiquated and meaningless term in a society with such values, deaf to the question of 'public virtues'.

The prevalent mentality today is that you, the subject, can choose infinitely. There is nothing that is permanent in your choices. The term 'definitive' or 'permanent' seems a horror. We want all options all the time. Likewise, the terms 'duty', 'virtue', and 'commitment' seem curiously old-fashioned. We have been liberated from them, as we have become liberated from every bond and institution handed down by history.

Political Man

Is there anything common in a society in which the individual only has a private interest? The extreme liberalism of the utilitarian tradition in England thought so: one can do everything which does not harm others, was their only principle. The common sphere of society was only that which one could not manage on one's own: police and defence.

Although this is perhaps one viable model of politics, it does not bring a community with it. It sees the political sphere as a management business. If the view of man is self-referential, i.e. the standard or measurement of all things resides in the individual, it is hard to find any scope for the traditional meaning of politics and law. The 'political' means that which concerns the *polis*, which is the political community. It concerns that which is *common*.

This is the classical Aristotelian view of politics, which offers something extremely different from the current self-referential view of man: here we learn that human nature is something very specific and that politics is the highest practical human activity, that the human being is unhappy unless he is contributing to the common good of society and, even more startling, that the human being is able to discern good from bad, right from wrong.

Man is not only a rational 'animal' who can communicate through language and who can reason, we read in the First Book of *The Politics*, but the human being is the only animal capable of making moral arguments. Animals can communicate, but they are unable to reason and they have no moral sense: 'Man is the only animal whom nature has endowed with speech ... and whereas mere voice is but an indication of pleasure and pain, the power of speech is intended to set forth the just and the unjust. And it is characteristic of man that he alone has any sense of good and evil, of just and unjust.'[2]

The human being can arrive at what is just and unjust through reason, and this is the very defining characteristic of him. What a tremendous difference there is between this assertion and the common assumption today that there are no moral truths and that even if they existed, they cannot be attained by reason. Yet, as we shall see, the political thinkers that forged European law and democracy not only assumed this, but also arrived at the just and unjust through reason.

In addition, man is a *social* animal, says Aristotle, which means that he can only fully realize himself as a human being in the social, i.e. the political sphere. This is startling to the modern self-referential person: am I only able to be fully human, fully myself as a *social* being?

The teleology of ancient philosophy is interesting, because we have forgotten what teleology implies. It means the science of *telos*, of the intention or purpose of a thing, or person, or institution. The intention is another word for *meaning*: there is a meaning behind creation; a meaning that can be discovered. This also means that there is an *ordo*, a connection between the parts, in life itself.

This sense of the metaphysical, of the order of things that exists prior to and independent of our knowledge and sense of it, is in my view extremely important in today's relativist universe. One assumes the possibility of metaphysics away as 'essentialism', but without realizing that the Western system of governance is based upon its existence. The notion of law as universally valid, as a set of general principles about right and wrong, is one example of this. If law can be anything to anyone, it is not law.

I therefore think that we must now deal with the radical question of what the human being is – anthropology – when we discuss European democracy today. Do we assume that the human being is only a self-interested

---

[2]   Aristotle, *Politics*, Book 1.

actor? Does he or she live only for his own satisfaction? Or is there more than this self-referential man – an ability to think politically along principled lines, about something called the 'common good'?

Even if one adheres to the self-referential view, there is a puzzle: how can one argue about right and wrong if there is no principle of justice to be known? How can one say that something is just or unjust? Clearly we mean more than just uttering the word; we mean that they refer to something that we describe as just or unjust. This is clear when we test the language use we have: can I say 'It is unjust to have a sailing boat'? Yes, I can say it, but it makes no sense. Can I say 'It is unjust to have slaves'? Yes, and it makes sense. Some may disagree, but it makes sense.

The latter statement is what Aristotle refers to when he says that the human being is able to reason politically and legally; that is, about right and wrong in *principled,* i.e. universal terms. If it is unjust to have a boat, it is unjust *tout court,* for everyone. This is a stupid assertion. But if it is unjust to have slaves, it is not only unjust in Europe, but also in Africa. The universalism of moral argument is an axiom: justice is generally just, or not just. But private preferences are just expressions of subjective taste, nothing more. I prefer a boat, you do not. The language of morals has no relation to such a preference, and it is therefore not at all relevant for the political sphere.

The notion of justice is laid down in the human being as a principle that can be discovered through reasoning of the kind that I exemplify above. We see immediately that the example of the sailing boat is nonsensical but that the example of slavery makes sense even when we may disagree on it.

This 'language' test is useful, for it allows us to define the political as distinct from the private interest. The principled terms of the debate indicate whether we deal with an issue that concerns us all; i.e. society or the polis; or whether we deal with an issue that is merely private, our own subjectivist interest. The concerns of self-referential man would then seem to belong, all of them, in the private sphere, as one here denies that there are principles that can be reasoned about. This diminishes the moral stature of politics.

Aristotle says, 'The true forms of government are those in which one governs with a view to the common good, but governments which rule with a view to the private interest ... are perversions.'[3]

Thus, not only is there a difference that can be defined between the political and the private, but this difference is also a *moral* one, not only a functional one. This assertion must seem extremely foreign to self-referential man. But here's the argument: the *telos* of Aristotle underlies his metaphysics and anthropology. Politics is not only the place where we aggregate private interests, such as deciding on having a common police instead of private guards because it is cost effective; but the political is moral, is different in that sense from the private interest. 'Every state is a community of some kind, and every community is established with a view to some good ... the state, which is the highest community of all, and which embraces the rest, aims at good in a greater degree than any other, and at the highest good.' [4]

The citizen is equipped with the ability to reason about justice, and this kind of reasoning is legal or political reasoning, contrasted with private reasoning, which does not concern the common good of all of society. In addition, the citizen must be educated in public virtue, which is the ability to think of the good of all and not only of private, personal interest. Again Aristotle emphasizes the moral qualities of politics proper: 'political society exists for the sake of noble actions – [for] political science the good [we seek] is justice, in other words, the common interest'.

The influence of the ancient political philosophy of Plato and Aristotle was decisive for Europe. St Thomas Aquinas

---

3   Aristotle, *Politics*, Book 2.
4   Aristotle, *Politics*, Book 1.

transmitted this knowledge and developed it into his own system of philosophy, which in turn exerted key influence throughout the ages. When Machiavelli marks the end of a Christian world view of Europe, he leaves this conception of politics. The same is true of the advent of the Westphalian state system from 1648 onwards, and the rise of positivism in interpretations of law. Yet the weakening of natural law arguments, which stand in the tradition of Aristotle and Thomas, continue as an alternative and contender.

The importance here of the Aristotelian tradition is not historical, but fundamental and contemporary to the argument of this book: only if the concept of human nature is intelligible, can the concept of human rights make sense. Alternatively, such rights are just reflections of majority will or some political process. But in that case how can they be 'inherent and inalienable'?

CHAPTER TWO

THE *RECHTSSTAAT* AS
DEMOCRATIC GUARANTEE

Tyranny refers to illegitimate or unjustified governance, and as such implies that the notion of justification or justice is meaningful. Tyranny is in classical political thought the usurpation of just rule, and is always presented as a perversion of good forms of government.

Democracy is one justified form of government where legitimacy emanates from the people. It can vote rulers down in a recall mechanism – rulers have to be accountable to the people. Democracy thus becomes tyrannical when this condition no longer obtains.

The legacy of liberal democracy is the normative model for most European states, and the only acceptable form of government in the West today is democracy. Even among self-professed sceptics who hold that no values or norms are universal, one is hard pressed to find a critic of democracy as such. All agree that this form of government is the best one, or at least the best there is to get in the absence of Platonic philosophers of the real kind. Democracy has come to stay and has developed in the West over the last 200–300 years. It is perhaps the only concept that is openly spoken of in Western politics as something that all should enjoy: one states that democracy must be instituted all over the world.

This form of government gradually included the whole

population over a certain age by extending suffrage to them; it contains representative institutions and holds periodic elections. Elected politicians are accountable to the electorate and can be 'recalled' in a new election. The government is accountable to parliament and there is a formal separation of powers in the legislative, the executive, and the judiciary. The constitution contains a Bill of Rights that lists fundamental rights for citizens – typically the right to life, liberty, property, the right to freedom of religion, association and free speech. The French constitution serves as a model for many European constitutions.

Typically these fundamental norms are regarded as 'higher' than other law and as so fundamental that they cannot easily be changed. Parliaments thus have elaborate and cumbersome procedures for changing constitutions. In some countries there are special constitutional courts that are in charge of interpreting what the constitution really says. In short, modern democracies are equipped with a *code of higher norms* that are supposed to be safe form political change and which are therefore insulated from the political process.

How were these norms generated? Where did they come from? In the French *code civil* they were simply decided on, as they were in other constitutions. For John Locke, the precursor of the modern democratic theory, the fundamental norms were self-evident. He held that there were some higher norms, but that they could not be reasoned about. But they were generated in the establishment of the 'social contract' and were thus not 'pre-political', belonging to man as a human being.

Modern democratic theory arose as part of social contract theory, and rests on three assumptions: first, that there are self-evident rights that belong to the individual and which should be protected by the constitution. These rights are however only postulated as such; they are not part of any argument about natural law. Second, the need for protection of these postulated rights is the reason for the creation of society in a social contract: in the state of nature man is thought to pursue self-interest in the form of power maximization but he needs to be protected from the others. Third, the state is a minimalist arbiter of pluralism among atomistic individuals: the state carries no values, politics is value-neutral. This institutional apparatus is what largely constitutes the legacy of modern democracy in the West.

More than a century ago, Mill, Tocqueville, and others were extremely concerned with the problem of majority tyranny. Mill's *On Liberty* (1859), the classic plea for liberty as the highest norm, agonizes over this issue:

> Protection against the tyranny of the magistrate is not enough; there needs to be protection also against the tyranny of the prevailing opinion and feeling ... against the tendency of society to impose its own ideas and practices as rules of conduct on those who dissent from them ... there is a limit to the interference of collective opinion with individual independence, and to find that limit is as indispensable to a good condition of human affairs as protection against political despotism.

On the one hand Mill saw the emergence of such a tyranny in democracy; on the other hand he could not find any remedy against it. This was because his premises were inconsistent: he postulated tolerance or liberty as the highest norm, saying that all is allowed that does not harm others. Politics is value-neutral, and only if you harm others should your freedom not be allowed. Yet he clearly held that some actions and norms are right and true, whereas others are wrong, but could not argue for this as he had no criterion of ranking value-judgements. The interpretation of what does harm and what does not ultimately rests with subjective opinion; since the state has to somehow decide here, it is unavoidable that politics embodies values and is about value-judgements.

Mill's problem is the same that we face today: tolerance or liberty is almost the only norm that democracy accepts, and is certainly the highest norm. We see this all the time in the public debate: new interest groups claim freedom from interference, claim tolerance for their interests, whatever the moral content of them. Morals or ethics is thought firstly to belong to the private sphere, secondly to be subjectivist. Value pluralism is the key premise.

Given this, how can fundamental norms be safeguarded, if at all? The procedure of democracy is some form of majority voting. Even constitutions can be changed by parliaments, although the procedures are more cumbersome than simple majority and take more time. However, the basic premise is that all political power is vested in the people, who in a social contract invest it in the institutions of state. Even the rights in the constitution come from the people, it would seem. But is this the case? Here we see an inherent inconsistency between the 'self-evident' character of fundamental individuals' rights, which are simply postulated, and the tendency today to usurp these rights by changing them through majority voting. I will return to empirical illustrations of this.

Classical democracy conceived of constitutional rights as being beyond the reach of majority procedure, although the constitutions could be changed. The judiciary was designed to be independent of the legislature in order to interpret and protect the constitution. However, the crux of the matter with regard to law and politics is not in variance of institutional design, but in the view of the origin of law. If everything is reduced to politics, there can be no protection from the application of the majority procedure to any principled question of human rights.

The autonomy of the private sphere is essential to democracy, and also the respect for civil disobedience in cases of conflict between an individual's norms and those of society. However, this is not enough. The state in the classical model was a minimal state whose task it was to deal with the tasks that the private sphere could not rationally solve by itself: army, police, postal, energy, and infrastructural services. The historical evolution of the state has led to a much larger public sphere, the development of the welfare state, and to state schools and often state churches. Whatever one's views on this development, it is clear that a sound democracy must contain a private sector with autonomous associations, a free market, and some distance between politics and the law, in addition to the premise of equality before the law as well as in political participation.

The major problem of modern Western democracy is the reduction of ethical questions to pragmatic, political ones. This is manifested in the lack of respect for human life in its non-utilitarian forms: unborn, handicapped, old, and sick; and in subjecting the taking of human life to pragmatic decision-making by majority procedure. This empirical development shows that the right to life enshrined in constitutions and international human rights documents carries little if any weight when pitted against feminist, economic, or other interests. More importantly, it shows that modern democracy is reduced to majority procedure. With tolerance as the only professed norm of the state, majority procedure becomes the essence of democracy. This development is inconsistent with the *Rechstsstaatstradition* which is based on the primacy of higher, unchangeable norms and independent institutions to safeguard them.

Abortion came to the fore in the public debate in Western democracies some thirty years ago. Everyone knew that abortions had always been performed in secrecy in the private sphere. Now women demanded that the state should perform them. Their argument was pragmatic: abortions will happen; they should be made 'safe'. Abortion was politicized, placed in the public-political sphere by feminist interest groups.

The terms of the debate had to be pragmatic because the liberal state cannot deal with 'value' questions. The state does not represent norms – the constitutional norms are just there to protect the individual from intrusion into his private sphere. The decision-making procedure in liberal democracy is majority decision. If however the terms of the debate are about universal norms of right and wrong, this procedure makes no sense. The political discussion thus has to be set in other terms. It has to be pragmatic.

In the case of the abortion debate, the fierce struggle which continues and which will continue is about the terms of the debate: if the question is 'Under which conditions can human life be taken?' one has to consider the constitutional norms of the right to life and the international instruments of human rights that state this as the highest norm. If the debate is cast in pragmatic terms, e.g. as a women's issue, this is not necessary. The abortion issue was decided when the terms of the debate were decided. But abortion represents a watershed in Western politics precisely because it exhibits a total cleavage in views on what is legitimate democratic politics and procedure.

This meant that ethics was defined away and that interest group politics won out. The same political process can be seen in the debate over euthanasia, which is now becoming politically prominent in Scandinavia, Australia, the US, and gradually in other Western states. The terms of the debate are being set in a very important process right now. For instance, one sees reports in the press on the increasing number of people who favour euthanasia, doctors who find it good for the patient, euthanasia as the right to choose, a new human right, etc. Interest group leaders actually say things like this: 'We do not have enough resources for all people; we must put priority on the young' (*Aftenposten*, March, 1996). There is in other words a process going on that seeks to pragmatize the issue so that it can easily be decided by majority procedure, and a concomitant process driven by interest groups that argues that abortion and euthanasia are new human rights.

A third issue that illustrates the inability to discuss ethical issues in ethical terms is that of using fetal tissue from induced abortion for medical purposes. In Norway an expert commission was set up to advise the government on this issue. Even the one bishop on the commission – a member of the Lutheran state church – turned out to be sympathetic to the government's proposal to use such tissue medically. The interesting aspect of this was however his way of reasoning: being against legalized abortion, he nonetheless argued for the use of fetal tissue because as abortion is allowed, one might as well make use of the results of it. He could not understand that there were problems with this argument from an ethical point of view – and in truth, his was a valid pragmatic argument: abortions will happen, let's make some use of them if we can. He could not understand that if he held that abortions were evil on principle, he would also have to hold that the ancillary act, using the fetal tissue, was evil and in fact might contribute to justifying the abortion itself.

These examples illustrate that the political discourse on ethical issues in liberal democracy is de facto pragmatic. Moreover, I have argued that it has to be pragmatic in order to fit with the central assumptions and institutions of liberal democracy: majority procedure, politics as 'value-free', and ethics as belonging to the private sphere. Yet it is also cast in 'rights' language – the right of women to abort, the right of old people to euthanasia, and so on.

But the 'rights' language is justified by pragmatic reasoning: because women have abortions, they are a right; and because many people accept euthanasia, it is a right. In this debate there is no discussion of which topics should belong in the private sphere – the strategy is to lift them into the public sphere. There is no hierarchy of principles for determining what is a common, and thus political problem, and what is not. We are faced with a completely confused debate, driven by interest groups.

How pervasive is this development? Abortion has become a 'right' in many Western countries, and continues to make 'progress' beyond Europe. Euthanasia is legalized in several countries already and I am convinced that it is only a question of time before it will be legal in many more. The 'rights' language used to make these policies more acceptable destroys the notion of fundamental constitutional rights by denying that there can be a hierarchy of rights and even that there are fundamental contradictions between rights, such as the right to life and the right to abortion.

Solutions?

I have argued that judged on the norms of constitutional-ism – that there are fundamental norms laid down in the constitution – contemporary democratic practice is often tyrannical. I say 'practice' because the institutions of liberal democracy have not been changed. One simply elevates the majority procedure to become the cornerstone of democracy and conveniently forgets the constitutional constraints on its exercise.

Further, there are no longer any shared 'values' or norms. The central premise of 'neutrality' on the part of the state in normative questions has of course always been a fiction. States act on norms in most of what they do as modern welfare states: they inculcate pupils with national and social norms in national school systems and they decide redistribution, health and foreign polices according to moral or normative standpoints.

The postulation of tolerance as the hallmark of the modern state is also fiction – it is a tolerance very selec-tively applied indeed. In questions of the taking of human life, as in abortion and euthanasia, one does not ask the logical ethical question of 'When is the taking of human life justified?'. Here the state has no normative stand even if its constitution explicitly states that a right to life exists. In these cases one avoids the normative discussion alto-gether and opts for a combination of pragmatism ('there is a need for abortion, abortions happen all the time') and selective 'rights' language (since abortions are favoured by a majority, a 'right' to abortion exists). The fallacy of inferring the existence of a right from empirical data is obvious, but hardly seen as such.

Here we are at the very core of the problem of democracy and value relativism. The two cannot meaningfully co-exist: where there is no set of fundamental norms underlying the political process democracies become, sooner or later, tyran-nies. I have pointed to the institutional inconsistencies within liberal democracy and the abuses of this system today. But the main problem is not institutional; it is ethical.

'Values' connote subjectivity: 'I accept abortion, you do not' – our value preferences differ. 'I accept euthanasia, you do not.' Again, simply a matter of different preferences. 'I accept genocide, you do not.'

But do we agree with this statement? No – here the reaction will be one of universal condemnation of killing for ethnic reasons. This shows two things: one, in dealing with the question of taking human life, the public is inconsistent because the question is not posed as one of principle, i.e. of ethics; and two, there is still a sound reaction in most people about genocide. They will not hesitate to condemn it as evil – but if values are simply subjective preferences, they ought logically to say 'I don't happen to like genocide, but if you do, you simply have other preferences than me.'

There thus exists a remnant of the language of morals in people. One reacts to dictatorships by calling them 'unjust', and thus retains some notion of justice. Justice was the basis for all legitimate government in the classical tradition, and justice requires principled reasoning. 'When can human life justifiably be taken?' Traditionally the answer was 'in self-defence'. The lost discourse on ethics today points back to a much richer European tradition of natural law, developed by Aristotle, rediscovered by St Thomas and further developed by him and medieval Christian thinkers. This discourse on politics disappeared at the time of Machiavelli with the triumph of the language of *Staatsraison*. Here one no longer discussed the relationship between 'might and right', but rather how to gain and keep 'might'. The question of justice as right ordering of society became obsolete.

We have seen that the utilitarianism of a Mill or Locke, coupled with the institutions of liberal democracy, invite the conclusion that 'might becomes right'. There is no higher norm outside politics. Likewise, with a Kantian approach one logically safeguards fundamental human rights but these rights do not come from man's nature; they remain a postulate that is in the interest of all in a civilized polity.

My contention is that only an anthropology that starts with the absolute dignity of the human being, of *any* human being – will do to ensure that persons will not be treated in a utilitarian manner. However, the problem is how to make the dignity of man apparent to all in societies where the word dignity no longer carries any meaning and where Nietzsche's *Umwertung aller Werte* is the point of departure.

CHAPTER THREE

THE DYNAMICS OF HUMAN RIGHTS POLITICS

Today's international politics increasingly deals with value questions. Human rights discourse is becoming the major form of political argumentation, nationally as well as internationally. Human rights instruments have proliferated, both as hard as well as soft law. Legalization as hard law, where there is a clear definition of states' obligations, is usually difficult to achieve in the human rights area, normally requiring consensus. For this reason those who want to change existing human rights norms mostly opt for soft law strategies, where one uses 'soft law to cast the normative net more widely, building as broad a coalition as possible. Strengthening the normative consensus and possibly the hardening of legal commitments is left to a more gradual process of learning' (Kahler, 2000: 679). In addition, we should note that most soft law obligations are obeyed by states. Non-compliance is rare in all inter-national regimes, even in the absence of coercive measures of enforcement. Chayes and Chayes (1995) investigated a number of international regimes where there were tenuous monitoring and implementation mechanisms, and found, like Koh (1997) in his major legal review, that international obligations are met by Western states, even in soft law cases. This indicates that the 'shaming' of non-compliance is feared, and that states do not want to be seen as unreliable international citizens. This is also why those who want to change human rights seek an inter-national strategy of soft law for the new norm above all else.

We also notice that the political agenda is often set by professional interest groups that invoke more or less well established international human rights norms as their basis of legitimacy. These actors we call 'norm entrepreneurs'. They are highly specialized, highly committed, and work exclusively for their cause. They are thus eminently equipped to succeed. Once an issue has been defined in human rights terms, it acquires a special legitimacy that is difficult to counter.

There are two areas of special concern to us where human rights discourse is used by strategic actors today: *the family* and *the right to life*. I recall that I noticed that in 1994 Norwegian politicians on the left started to consider the notion of the family to be a problem. This situation had arisen from the UN's Year of the Family. These politicians started to talk about the 'various forms of the family' every time there was some event related to the UN Year of the Family. I remember that I was very disturbed by this, but I did not at the time realize that this was part of an international action movement on this issue. Likewise, when I negotiated for the Holy See at the Beijing conference in 1995, my Scandinavian and Dutch colleagues were especially eager to highlight the number of maternal deaths resulting from illegal abortions. This was a very high number indeed, and I wondered how they could arrive at it, given the secrecy surrounding illegal abortions. But it was the key way in which they tried to set the agenda. This was of course a way to make legal abortion a medical solution to a perceived problem of immense proportions – making safe what was already unsafe.

As we shall see later, both these issues have been defined in human right terms: abortion as a human right for women; and the right to form a family as an individual right, regardless of sex.

In this intervention I analyse how norms about new human rights are created at the international level and how these are transmitted and used strategically to influence the domestic level. The two examples I mention are salient ones that I will use throughout. At the end I discuss how natural law definitions of the family and of the right to life can successfully be promoted, using the very same tools that the adversaries of natural law are using.

International Norm-Creation in Human Rights

The post-war period is the era of human rights. The UN Declaration of Universal Human Rights of 1948 is based on a global consultation process, specifically taking into account the experiences of all religions and regions. Although not legally binding – it is only a declaration – it is regarded in international law as authoritative. All later human rights instruments are based on the formulations in the declaration. As regards our two cases; the declaration specifies that 'everyone has the right to life' and that 'the family is the basic unit of society'. These definitions are fully in accordance with natural law definitions.

Subsequent to the declaration, we have the two conventions of 1966 on civil and political, social and economic human rights. These are legally binding, although there is no court to enforce them. Also here we find the same definitions of our two cases.

Then we should be aware of the European Convention on Human Rights (ECHR) of 1950. This convention is implemented by the European Court of Human Rights in Strasbourg, and is adhered to by forty-one member states of the Council of Europe today. The formulations in the convention are the same as in the Universal Declaration on our cases, but it should be noted that case law on what the 'right to life' means has not gone against the abortion legislation in member states. The rulings of the European Court of Human Rights are implemented and have direct effect in states where the ECHR is incorporated into national law, which means most member states of the Council of Europe today.

When invoking human rights in these two areas – family definitions and family rights – the right to life and the dignity of the human person – we should rely on the texts of the above documents, especially the most authoritative, viz. the Universal Declaration of Human Rights. Later instruments in the UN system have largely been based on these definitions when the document is a convention, although the language has not always been clear. Therefore one should adhere to the most authoritative documents, and not necessarily the newest ones. The Universal Declaration can arguably be invoked as the most important one from which other, later documents must simply follow. Naturally this view is met by the argument that human rights evolve, and that therefore what comes later is more attuned to progress. I will deal with this later.

But these formulations and definitions, consistent with natural law, are contested in several ways today, and therefore we need to study the way in which it has been sought to change them.

New Actors: The Norm Entrepreneurs

First, new actors that are transnationally organized use whatever is convenient for their cause. The NGOs (non-governmental organizations) that promote alternative family forms or abortion will use the Beijing Final Document instead of the Universal Declaration, although the former has no legal or authoritative status whatsoever. What matters is simply to find some UN document that can be invoked because UN documents carry legitimacy in most states around the world. The legal scholars Abbott and Snidal notice that 'soft law' – non-binding international documents – often carry much weight and are in fact treated by interested actors as if they were hard law: this applies directly to the UN conferences in the last decade (Abbott and Snidal, 2000). In fact, aiming for soft law bases for new norms is a preferred strategy because its status in the international political system is so ambiguous.

Soft law instruments as well as legalization at the international level have increased very much in the last decades. Legalization is a strategy to create binding norms which carries more weight and legitimacy than mere soft law, but which is harder to achieve and which requires member state approval and often consensus (Keohane et al., 2000). Thus, soft law is the preferred tool for those who want to change norms (Goldstein, 2000; Abbot et al., 2000).

Further, the growth of transnational advocacy networks is very important to the understanding of value politics today (Risse-Kappen, 1995). The growth of national NGOs is to be found in single-issue areas, and these groups easily network in horizontal ways. Modern communications help this organizational form (Kamarck and Nye, 1999). NGOs typically seek out causes where it is easy to present the issue as a singularly good thing, as an improvement or progress, and use human rights language as mode of argumentation and as justification. First, something is defined as a human right, e.g. abortion. Then abortion is justified because it is a human right.

Keck and Sikkink (1998) have done extensive analysis of such transnational advocacy networks. They describe the strategies of these actors as a *pincer movement*: first, the establishment of the new or redefined norm is sought at the international level. Here UN conferences are the best arenas because they carry most legitimacy, but also other arenas may be attractive in specific regions. The norm change sought is typically that of soft law, which does not require member state consensus.

Once a text change has been established, it can be invoked at the national level as authoritative. The national NGOs work at this level all the time, seeking to prepare the public debate and public opinion. The invoking of the norm from the international onto the national level is successful only if there is some preparedness for its reception (Cortrell and Davis, 1996). This can be created by the *elite policy level*, where civil servants incorporate SOPs (standard operating procedures) in bureaucratic routines that have political significance, such as defining the abortion pill as 'emergency contraception', as has been done by the WHO (World Health Organization) and then, by national bureaucracies.

In order to succeed in doing this, one preferably needs both some scientific basis (which can be had for any argument today), as well as some text in an international document. The important role of scientific evidence has been studied especially under the aegis of the environment, in the case of climate change, which has been essentially contested for a long time. Haas has shown how 'epistemic communities' – important groups of experts who agree on what the 'state of the art' in their field concludes – form to support a scientific viewpoint, and that such communities exert major influence on both policy-makers and public opinion (Haas, 1992 and 1993). There are no systematic studies of medical science in this regard: are there epistemic communities regarding homosexuality and gender issues? Do psychiatrists basically agree on whether homosexuality is learned behaviour or innate? Do they agree on whether children need both male and female roles models in the upbringing? From Soviet history we know that all science can be manipulated, but the interesting question is to what extent political actors in Western democracies try to create such epistemic communities in these areas today. It is clear that any position can find its scientific 'evidence' in the global marketplace, but it is politically significant if some actors, such as NGOs, actively seek to create scientific strongholds for their views. We know that the tobacco industry has supported medical research on smoking – a case in Denmark was just exposed – and there is every reason to believe that other types of interest groups also try to mobilize science on their side.

Thus, there are essentially three sources of authority for political arguments about norms and values: international approval; popular, domestic approval; and scientific evidence. Thus, new norms can also be seemingly generated from below, through agenda setting of the public debate. NGOs are of course expert at this. Finnemore and Sikkink lay out how the invocation of the international norm happens while the same norm is being supported from below, so that one arrives at both democratic legitimacy as well as being 'told' by the UN or some other international body to follow the norm (Finnemore and Sikkink, 1998).

In the period after the norm has received some international recognition in some text, the advocacy networks work intensely to create a 'cascade': the norm should be seen and debated everywhere. Thus, one overcomes resistance to the norm by becoming familiar with it, and one thinks after a while that the norm is both just, the result of progress, and natural. The present process toward creating 'homosexual families' is in the 'cascade' phase: there are many initiatives for debate in every Western country, and those who are against this concept are seen as being against progress, tolerance, and human rights for homosexuals. There is a very agile and competent transnational advocacy network at work here: in UN conferences we have seen efforts to insert 'sexual orientation' and 'various forms of the family' for about a decade now, carried out especially by feminist groups who have access to the UN conferences. At the same time there has been a very systematic work at national level by homosexual groups, arguing in human rights language. The first step was the legal recognition of partnership; the second step is legal recognition of family rights on a par with the normal family. In Holland legislation on this was passed recently. The new EU charter on human rights has, for example, a wording on the family that departs from the one quoted above which has been standard and which mentions that men and women have the right to marry and establish a family. In the EU text it simply says that 'everyone has the right to form a family'.

Thus, the interaction between the international and national level is an important one where the two levels consolidate each other. A norm invoked from the international level confers legitimacy (Hurd, 1999) – a key variable in modern transparent politics – and a norm seen to emerge from below likewise confers the most important source of legitimacy of all, viz. democratic legitimacy. In the case of 'homosexual families', we can record how polls are taken at regular intervals, showing gradual increases in acceptance for this concept. Once the numbers approach 50%, the norm is well grounded. Politicians will then follow suit, based on their respect for popular opinion (or fear thereof!). The campaign is successfully completed when the new norm is embedded in national legislation and practice. At this point it is part of national practice and perhaps law, and that makes it almost unassailable. The right to abortion has been on Norwegian law books for thirty years now, and public opinion is almost totally in favour of this. It takes exceptional skill and courage as well as independent thinking to advocate deviation from the law of one's own state. The status of international law, especially soft law, is much more tenuous; it can be applied or invoked, it can also be totally ignored in most cases. Few international instruments have enforcement and even monitoring mechanisms, and in the case of soft law, it is obvious that its role depends entirely on whether 'norm entrepreneurs' decide to use it.

Both national and international organizations and bureaucracies may be actors in norm change – they are 'norm entrepreneurs', as Sikkink calls them, and I am tempted to recall that modern warlords are called 'conflict entrepreneurs'. These strategic actors are often operators between the national and international levels, and we know that they wield important influence on negotiations in international conferences, working in networks of transnational civil servants.

There are several success stories of how transnational advocacy networks have achieved their goals. For instance, the international campaign to ban landmines (ICBL) managed to get a core set of states to support its cause, and the convention on the use and stockpiling of landmines actually achieved hard law status – it is a legally binding convention. In this process the NGOs were the major actors in setting the agenda and launching a process, against the persistent opposition of the US. One can also mention the anti-apartheid movement in South Africa, where again the US was opposed to the claims for abolition, but was gradually forced to change its national position (Klotz, 1995). It is obvious that in order to succeed in such norm change, one has to have a 'good cause' in the sense that it can be easily put in terms of a human right, and preferably in terms of good vs. bad. In the two cases mentioned above, this was easy. But in addition to a 'good cause' that easily persuades, one has to have a number of other political resources: a well-functioning transnational network, access to press and media, access to the relevant international arenas, access to favourable scientific knowledge when necessary; and ability to stay the course during the period of international norm establishment and its domestic diffusion and embedding. In the two cases mentioned above, it was critical to the transnational NGO to get a set of core states on board. States are still the main actors of international politics. Once a 'coalition of the willing' has been established, this tends to attract also other states which do not want to be seen as laggards. If a coalition really gets started – as it was in the landmine case – then no state, apart from those that really have a vital national interest at stake, wants to be left behind.

New International Arenas for Norm-Creation Proliferate

The number of international arenas for norm-creation has increased significantly in the latest decade. A plethora of UN conferences on normative issues have been held: on the environment, on population and development, on women, on social policy, on small arms and light weapons, and on racism. In addition, there are very many other forums where international norms are debated and developed: in the whole UN 'family' of organizations, in the OSCE (Organization for Security and Cooperation in

Europe), the Council of Europe (COE), the WTO (World Trade Organization), OECD (Organization for Economic Cooperation and Development), etc.

Who are interested parties here? The states, but only the states with a particular interest in an issue. States have far too much to do to invest major energy in such conferences apart from the states which take a particular interest in the issue area. Thus, the most interesting actors here often are the NGOs which drive single-issue causes, such as feminism or the environment. In an international organization, some states are leaders, others are followers, and the rest are often passive. At the UN, there are two Western leaders, the US and the EU, and one non-Western leader, the G-77 (which now has 144 members). The US is the only superpower in the world which uses the UN when it needs legitimacy; otherwise not. Being a superpower, it can afford to refuse to pay its UN dues. Everyone knows that the UN would amount to nothing without the US. The EU has also become a major power: as well as its members, it is usually supported by all the candidate states, by the aspiring states beyond this, and by the European Economic Area states such as Norway and Iceland.

G-77 is an amorphous actor which is important because it gathers such a large number of states.

At the UN, the positions of these three actors basically determine an outcome. But the UN 'family' organizations and their bureaucracies also play a major part. Often these actors have the expert knowledge that states lack, and influence the draft texts because they write them. State power depends on staying power, engagement, and discernment. An international organization will seek to enhance its own power, and state control is often very slack indeed. Also, at the UN one estimates that about sixty ambassadors never ask for instructions from their capitals. Democratic control from national legislatures is largely an illusion.

There is no logic that is agreed upon regarding the relationship between the UN and other international bodies and the nation-state. Often there is deliberate ambiguity: I was going to address the UN commission on the status of women when I was Norwegian state secretary, and had written my own text. One delegation member – a civil servant sympathetic to abortion – said: 'What will happen if you speak about the right to life in your intervention? If Parliament in Norway sees that, what about our abortion law? You represent a minority government.' This rather direct threat made me call the Foreign Office, asking what to do: after all, Norway hails the Universal Declaration which speaks about exactly the right to life. The answer was 'go ahead' – we support the right to life in our UN speeches. No one has ever reflected on the total discrepancy between the national and the international level in Norwegian politics here – or have they just remained true to the postmodern dictum that logic is an unknown?

So I highlighted the right to life in my talk.

Sovereignty is Changing

To become less important, and international, norms acquire more legitimacy, power, and status. Old-style sovereignty, meaning non-intervention, is simply no longer accepted by leading First World states. Only pariahs like Algeria, Cuba, North Korea and the like insist on this type of sovereignty. Thus, human rights as universal standards have become much more acceptable as a reason for intervention in the last decades. This development is well documented, ranging from legal supremacy of human rights law (Rosas, 1993 and 1995) to studies of the radically changing nature of sovereignty (Chayes and Chayes, 1995; Koh, 1997; Donnelly, 1988; Fox, 1997; Lyons and Mastanduno, 1995). Krasner has aptly called his book *Sovereignty: Organized Hypocrisy* (1999), because there is a great deal of absolute hypocrisy in the actual practice of sovereignty. Those who look for clear rules of who is sovereign in which issue area – the national or the international level – have to look elsewhere – international law and international politics are

often deliberately ambiguous here. What is legally codified may of course be defined clearly, but that is only the
first step: is there any application, and if so, is it consistent? As de Gaulle reputedly said, 'International treatises
are like girls and roses, they last while they last.' In the
sphere of soft law it is even worse: here it is very much
up to the 'norm entrepreneurs' to design a political strategy. Do the Beijing conclusions bind anyone? Not legally,
but they may nonetheless be politically important to the
extent of ending up in national law books. How? Through
a carefully designed political strategy. In a state where
no one is interested in these conclusions and where there
are no actors to drive the issue, not a soul will take an
interest. And had the conclusions been legally binding,
no one would ever know or feel any impact, for who
would enforce them?

But the importance of human rights is an undeniable
fact which has led to major interventions in other states in
the post-cold war period. Military interventions are also
increasingly justified by humanitarian concerns, judging
by the new practices of the Security Council in the last
decade (Matláry, 2001). People across the Western world
now regard human rights as more important than state
sovereignty – which is a fact that should please Catholics,
who have never regarded the nation-state as the ultimate
source of authority, political or otherwise.

New Sources of Political Power Gain in Importance

The mechanisms of foreign policy have increasingly come
to ressemble those of ordinary, domestic politics. The
NGOs, the media, and citizens act and launch initiatives,
demanding accountability from foreign policy-makers.
Thus, foreign policy-makers have to react and to act. They
are no longer insulated from the domestic political
process.

With this 'democratization' of foreign policy, there has
arisen a great interest in human rights. The legitimization

of policy which is offered is increasingly that of human rights and democracy. We 'intervene' in other states in terms of media support, human rights dialogues, party cooperation to develop multi-party systems, 'shaming' of recalcitrant states in international forums, economic boycotts of non-democratic regimes, and so on. The Norwegian government has, for example, funded the Serbian opposition for several years, including the opposition press. Likewise, in states which are still repressive we fund similar institutions in a discrete manner, often in order to enable the opposition to launch a successful bid for change. This kind of foreign policy is right and good seen with the eyes of universal human rights, but it is completely contrary to the norm of non-intervention.

There is a long list of such policy tools, and the list of states that do not claim to be democracies today, is short indeed. Foreign policy seems to gravitate more and more towards such values, at least in terms of the justification policy given by policy-makers.

There is a renewed discussion about power in the post-cold war period. As Ingebritsen notes, 'international relations ... have begun to focus on how states exercise influence in ways that do not conform to strictly economic or military capabilities. Instead of viewing the international system as fragmented and anarchic, a new wave of scholarship examines how states become socialized into an international community or society'.[1] Nye has developed this theme, coining the term 'soft power' as the power that persuades rather than coerces, and argues that the US is also the leading 'soft power' holder in 'hard' fields like security policy, where the future belongs to those that command technology, education, and institutional flexibility. In the military field, they argue, it is the US that leads because of its ability to process and gain knowledge through sophisticated systems of intelligence collection, surveillance, and reconnaissance. This enables

---

[1]   Ingebritsen, 1999, p. 2.

the actor to 'use deadly violence with greater speed, range, and precision',[2] such as was evidenced in the Gulf War. The authors predict that with the leading edge in communication technology, the US will be able, 'without commensurate risk, to thwart any military action'.[3] Indeed, this is what we may be witnessing in the effort to create a shield against missile attacks.

Nye provides a very useful continuum of types of power (Nye, 1995). On the most familiar end, we find coercive power. This power gives you the ability to command others to follow your will. Military power is the key power source here, but economic power also counts. Sanctions are one instance of this. But at the other end of the continuum we find co-optive power. This is the power to make others agree with you and desire the same things as you do. They may be induced to do so; through light pressures such as creating incentive structures that they follow, or through 'shaming' and open criticism, or threats of such. There are many diplomatic ways of arm twisting.

But as we move towards the right side of the continuum, we find 'agenda-setting' and 'attraction'. These power sources may be even stronger; when you really manage to define a problem and set its agenda, you then have control of the decision-making process to a great extent. But still your power may be based on light coercion and pressures, although they are hidden as part of a 'democratic' decision-making procedure. The most powerful situation is when you persuade others to think like you do and strive for the same goals. When they accept your problem definition and the premises for the subsequent decision-making, you have exercised the most important power resource: the other person is convinced that you are right, and he internalizes your views. You have exercised the power of persuasion.

With command power, you must assume that the other

[2]   Ibid., p. 23.
[3]   Ibid., p. 24.

will turn against you and disobey you when you no longer threaten him. With co-optive power, you obtain your goal – to make the other do as you want – without pressures and threats. It is obvious that this type of power is much more effective than the first.

There is nothing new in this. Power has always come in different kinds. Throughout history women have often only been able to exercise power through their men, in an indirect and covert fashion. Today there are luckily other power resources available to women.

Karl Marx's analysis of structural power is eminent: power that you need not exercise is more effective than active power use. If you own the town, you need not use the ballot to get elected – it is enough to throw your weight around. The Norwegian political scientist Stein Rokkan formulated this in the famous phrase: 'Votes count, resources decide'. Structural power is embedded in social situations – everyone knows who is powerful, and they behave in anticipation of this. When journalists do not write about certain subjects, they exercise self-censorship because someone in that society has communicated that doing otherwise will lead to punishment.

The unseen power is hard to challenge. It may be personal power over others in the work place, it may be power exercised over economic resources and jobs, and it may be military and economic power in the international system which determine who is a big power and who is not. When a big power moves a little, the small states jump. Some call it the 'dinosaur effect'.

But what is new today, says Nye, is the salience of co-optive or 'soft' power. He argues that the US continues to be the most powerful state because it succeeds in exercising 'soft' power in addition to traditional 'hard' power: 'Soft co-optive power is just as important as hard command power. If a state can make its power legitimate in the eyes of others, it will encounter less resistance to its wishes. If its culture and ideology are attractive, others will more willingly follow ... In short, the universalism of a country's culture and its ability to establish a set of favourable rules and institutions that govern areas of international activity are becoming more important in world politics today.'[4]

Soft power resources enhance the promotion of values such as human rights and democracy. This is because soft power is typically exercised in public, as part of public diplomacy. Also, the actors using soft power are not only states, but also NGOs, media and international organizations and regimes. The issues raised by the latter often concern international norms and issue areas such as human rights, the environment, humanitarian standards, detente, and so forth. The point of departure is the individual and his rights, much more than states and their prerogatives. Multilateral diplomacy concerns itself with common interests or common problems, not with national interests in a narrow sense.

Also, in the public sphere the justification given for a national position is not a crude self-interest. An explanation must be given, preferably related to scientific reasoning. When discussing and negotiating in multilateral diplomacy, the public explanation is never blunt national interest. There needs to be *justification* for policy stances which is part of the general discourse. If an international treaty is not followed, there is an expectation for an explanation that refers to a general phenomenon. One cannot say that one simply does not care to implement it.

Thus, the logic of public diplomacy is such that principled and general reasons must be given. These must be relevant to the issue in order to be seen as legitimate by the other parties. Many times the real motivations are naturally traditional national interests, but even so this has to be hidden.

The old-style sovereignty is seen as illegitimate among the states that count in the world, i.e. the Western world. Norms are universal – as natural law adherents are the first to admit – but there is less and less agreement on the

---

[4]   Ibid., p. 33.

basis of such norms. Here we have to go back to first principles of philosophy.

Political Argumentation Must be Persuasive

It succeeds when it is couched in terms of individual rights, often presented as progressive evolution in human understanding and tolerance. The idea of a human nature is regarded by the postmodern Western person as a bygone essentialist position, and constructivism is the reigning fad. Constructivism has become the implicit assumption for modern social and political life. It means that, for example, sex is malleable and that there is no masculine or feminine; just learnt social roles. Even hetero and homo sexuality is just a subjective 'preference' or 'orientation' which can be changed at will. It is obvious that such an anthropology has immediate and profound implications for the definition of the family. It implies that there can be no such definition, as a definition must refer to recognizable classes of fact. It further implies that fatherhood and motherhood are social roles that can be assumed by either sex as they are not innate to the male and the female.

Constructivism as an ontology underlies the feminist movement and is the very basis for its *telos*, which is liberation from learned and imposed roles. If motherhood is a learned role, then recognition of this fact leads to liberation. Likewise, fatherhood becomes synonymous with the patriarchal family. To call something 'natural' becomes a politically repressive strategy aimed at perpetuating the institution of the traditional family. Thus, without the ideological foundation based on constructivism, both feminism and the homosexual movement – both of whom attack the natural family – would lack its very dynamic. Feminists would have to acknowledge that there exists something essentially feminine and masculine, while homosexuals would have to accept that the family arises from a natural biological union of male and female who beget children, and that whatever they call their own cohabitation and partnerships, it cannot be called a family.

Thus, constructivism as the basis of modern politics is the major challenge to those who uphold natural law. In the international instruments I have mentioned, we find definitions that accord with natural law. But they are of course challenged by a philosophy, almost always only implicit, which denies the very possibility of definitions.

This brings us directly to the realm of political argumentation. The concept of law is based on the ability to define, rather permanently, what the law prescribes or forbids. This presupposes the concept of human nature, which in turn is a perennial concept: by definition human nature does not change. It either is or is not what we attribute to it. But the modern world does not believe in human nature and in the recognition of vices as well as virtues. Rather the personal freedom of all is the basis of modern politics. This redefines the concept of tolerance to be one of acceptance of everything that is seen as legitimate at the present moment. When we refer to the Universal Declaration, we at the same time imply that the human experience that informed it is consistent with human nature. But for someone who thinks that the present moment represents human progress, and that history is simply outdated, this declaration can have no authority because the very concept is invalid. But on such a view all norms become expressions of mere power, and there can be no standard by which to measure these norms. The paradox here is that the 'norm entrepreneurs' always present their case as 'good', 'progressive' and an improvement on what was before. But how can they know that something is good or an improvement if they have no objective standard or criterion of comparison?

Despite the logical flaws here, I think we can safely conclude that the contemporary political process around norm change is very unprincipled, but that is part of political life. What we see, however, is that such norm change is facilitated by modern communications, views of sovereignty, the pervasiveness of soft law, and by the strategic action potential of non-state groups.

My last comment is that the triumph of human rights in the modern world is good news indeed. It means that natural law precedes state sovereignty, and that states cannot hide behind their borders. It also means that the long tradition of the Catholic Church in political theory and social teaching can come to its full fruition, not as theory, but as practical, implemental politics. This is indeed a major change since the treaties of Westphalia in 1648 which put state sovereignty above all other norms.

PART TWO:

HOW MIGHT BECOMES

HUMAN RIGHT

CHAPTER FOUR

HUMAN RIGHTS IN GLOBAL POLITICS AND BUSINESS

In the debate following the Kosovo air campaign, it was argued that there is a shift from interest-based to value-based foreign policy, The West intervened militarily to protect human rights, it was said. Some called it a humanitarian intervention, a concept much in vogue at present. Yet others maintained that this was plain, old-fashioned interest-based policy, seeking to consolidate balances of power between the great powers in the Balkans.

But they were hard pressed to identify exactly whose and which interests were being served by the risky and costly campaign. It was simply not plausible to maintain that the US did this to enhance its power in the area, or that other NATO allies had this intention. As a partial explanation it seemed right, but it was not the basic explanation.

It is not news that there is a tension between human rights, by nature universal, and the central defining characteristic of the international system, which is the principle of sovereignty.

Historically sovereignty has many meanings. Mostly we associate it with the treaties of Westphalia of 1648, which ended the Thirty Years War by laying down the principle that the ruler decides within his territory. In a Europe where feudalism had defined power structures non-territorially and where the Catholic Church exercised both temporal and spiritual power, there had not been such a thing as the nation-state. Power or authority had been defined along functional, not territorial lines. But the long struggle between emperor and Church on the one hand and the Protestant princes on the other was won in favour of the latter.

The Westphalia treaty text made it clear that

> to prevent for the future any differences arising in the politick state, all and everyone of the Electors, Princes and States of the Roman Empire, are so establish'd and confirm'd ... that, by virtue of this present Transaction: that they never can or ought to be molested therein by any whomsoever upon any manner of pretence. (art. LXIV)

In addition it was made clear that these principalities had the right to close agreements between them and with other states, thus making the territorial border the main political variable. The theorists of the new order, such as Jean Bodin, referred to this as the fact that the sovereign or prince is not subject to any other's command.

This principle of concentration of power inside a given territory became the cornerstone of the international system. It makes 'non-intervention' the central norm, as expressed in e.g. the UN Charter's paragraphs 2.4 and 2.7 which state that the use of force against another state is impermissible, apart from the cases where military power is used in self-defence or where 'international peace and security' is threatened. In the 1990s, however, the Security Council defined several such conflicts as threats – Somalia, Bosnia, and to some extent Kosovo.

The Westphalian principle says that the state has a monopoly on the use of force both inside and outside of the state. On the outside, the state shall refrain from attacking other states and is obliged to protect its own territory, mostly by having an army. On the inside, the state has the monopoly on the use of force vis-à-vis its citizens.

We can at the outset conclude that there exists a tension between the principles of human rights and non-intervention: on the one hand, we agree that the individual has rights that are universal and thus cut across borders; on the other hand, we accord the states themselves such rights, by accepting the Westphalian principle that the state has all power over its citizens within its territory. How can these principles be reconciled if at all?

Principles are one thing, practice another. The emphasis we put on principles gives them life and weight. Thus, what we observe in the present period is that the international community places relatively more weight on the human rights logic than on the state logic – albeit selectively, one may add.

But does this mean that power goes out when values come in? No. The change is that there are new forms of power that become more salient than old forms of power. Hard power – military power – becomes less usable and less attractive with the end of the cold war. The thesis that values matter more now than before is therefore basically limited to the Western world, and to those states that wish to enter into Western-dominated institutions.

But values are not means; they are ends. Power is a means to an end, regardless of which one. Thus, before discussing the values which I argue are more salient now than before, I want to discuss the new forms of power.

Power

Power is the key concept in any analysis of politics. Power is the means to reach one's ends. The ends vary greatly. Sometimes the ends are the values of democracy, rule of law and human rights. Sometimes the ends are quoted to be such, but this is just a cover up for other, more sinister motives. And sometimes the ends are conquest or simply to achieve more influence internationally.

A great deal of confusion arises when we confuse means and ends. There is nothing negative about power – it is the necessary means to achieve any goal. A standard definition tells us that power is the ability to make others do what you want. But power is much more than this – it is also the ability to make others accept your own visions, values, and goals. There are thus many types of power, and we need different types of power for different goals.

Values

The values I have mentioned are human rights, democracy, and the rule of law. Human rights, one could say, are the values proper, the ends of politics. Democracy and the rule of law are political conditions for the realization of human rights.

Human rights are basically a phenomenon of the post-war period in the Western world. They include the traditional political and civil rights, as well as the social and political rights: the right to life and security of person, the right to religious freedom, freedom of assembly, press freedom, freedom to own property and to marry and create a family, the right to work and to a just wage, to social benefits and to political participation. In the major human rights document, the Universal Declaration of Human Rights of 1948, there is an explicit mention of the form of political system that corresponds to human rights, viz. democracy. The 'will of the people' is to be the basis of politics, and 'all are equal before the law'. This is the rule of law, the integral part of liberal democracy.

The connection between human rights and democracy, including the rule of law, may not seem obvious. But when we examine the values underlying democracy, we find exactly this central concept: equality. This is both an equality before the law as well as an equality in terms of rights to political influence and to social and economic benefits, thus corresponding to democracy as a political form.

If we take a closer look at democracy's logic, we see that

the central value on which it is based is equality, and that this value is also the basis of human rights.

Aristotle said that politics is the highest practical science where one learns to be a virtuous person, ready to serve others without self-interest in mind, because by nature man is a 'social and political animal' – in Greek, a *zoon politikon*. We can only realize our full humanity in social relationships, and politics is where we develop public virtues such as justice, which is about what is right and wrong.

Later Thomas Aquinas repeated this, in the thirteenth century, and laid the foundation for modern democracy by stating that all men are fundamentally equal. They therefore cannot be subjected to unjust rulers. As we know, much later democratic forms of government developed in Europe, founded on this revolutionary equality.

This is of critical importance for the question of values.

Equality means that people are equal before the law, but also that they have a certain economic equality. They cannot have dignity and freedom unless they also have some economic basis. For those who cannot work, or cannot find work, this places an obligation on society to provide.

We see immediately that democracy itself is founded on a value, equality, which implies not only rights, but duties.

Equality, to be realistic, means that the weak and the sick also have a right to participate and to live in society. These values correspond to what we call human rights in modern language. The political rights and the socio-economic rights that form the basis for equality are intimately connected, in national as well as international society. The UN passed two legally binding conventions in 1966: one on political and civil rights, the other on social and economic rights. The two sets of human rights hang together, and can only be realized in the form of a political system that promotes equal votes, press freedom, assembly freedom, and so on.

It thus makes sense to speak of human rights and democracy as values as they are so intimately connected.

Democracy without respect for human rights becomes an empty procedure, and human rights in a dictatorship hardly make sense.

Inside the nation-state of the West there has been democracy cum rule-of-law for more than a hundred years; indeed, the Western state is built on the gradual evolution of this form of government. It is thus not news that human rights correspond to the current form of government, and that there is no essential tension between them in principle – albeit there often is in practice. The law-based international human rights instruments have therefore been compatible with national systems of governance in the West. However, national policy has not often been thought of or discussed as human rights policy, which has mostly been the terms of discourse on the international level, not the national level. In most states, governments have simply assumed that they fulfilled all human rights.

What is the connection between soft power and values? We argue that values not only become increasingly salient as justifications in foreign policy, but also that they are real reasons for action, real motivations; at least in some cases. Furthermore, we argue that even in hard power interventions, like Kosovo, massive human rights violations have become real forces of action. But it is nonetheless probable that the most interesting connection exists between soft power resources and values.

This has to do with justifications. When human rights are invoked as reasons for policy action, it is mostly a policy by a state or a group of states aimed at conditions in a third state.

Ethics and Human rights Under Globalization

In my native Norwegian tongue there are two words that connote ethical integrity: One is *hel ved* – 'whole wood', meaning a log that has no cracks in it; thus, no weak point. The other term is even more telling: *kjernekar* literally means a fellow – *kar* – who has a core, a *kjerne*. This term is commonly used, but when one asks what the core consists of, people are baffled. They all know what this quality is – integrity, honesty, solidity in things ethical – yet few know how to describe it beyond that. Either you know it, or you don't.

As a business leader today you have to be *kjernekar* or take a high risk of failure. A recent Burston-Marsteller survey of top leaders in Scandinavia shows – to my surprise and I suppose to yours – that ethics is regarded as one of the most important qualities of senior managers. 'If the ability of sound ethical judgement is not there, it can have disastrous consequences for the company,' says Claus Sonberg of Burston.[1] He thinks the Enron scandal and several Scandinavian cases lately account for this realization.

I think there is ample evidence that basically, only crisis teaches a lesson. It was only after the fact that Shell took a major interest in human rights in Nigeria, and the story repeats itself in several cases where I have advised Norwegian leaders on how to hedge against crisis. They come to ask advice only *post factum*; when the press has chased them out of the 'no comment' mode. By then it is too late to take charge of a process; only damage limitation remains, if that.

While insecurity mounts in the world, both in physical and political terms, you also have to rely more and more on your own ethical judgement. The nation-state is no longer there to provide a normative framework for right and wrong, and churches who do continue to provide such, are not listened to as secularization advances. And as ethical frameworks disappear the ethical accountability that you are supposed to be held to, becomes more present: stakeholders of various kinds demand that you are a promoter of all good things: human rights, Corporate

---

[1] *Dagens Næringsliv* (Oslo financial paper), 8.12.2003. 'Etikk viktigere enn penger' (Ethics is more important than money).

Social Responsibility (CSR), good governance in host countries, etc. The list is endless. You are under scrutiny by the media, specialized single-interest NGOs, hostile competitors, shareholders who sometimes buy shares strategically to oust you, clients and consumers. You cannot hide behind national ethical codes in the global firm. You are quite alone in trying to figure out what kind of ethical platform you must acquire. Life for an executive is indeed, like the Hobbesian subject in *Leviathan*, often 'nasty, brutish, and short'.

A very perceptive article in the *Financial Times* reads: 'Survival in the corporate jungle demands political skill',[2] as chief executives need to be alert to stakeholder demands in a new way that requires a 'permanent campaign'. They live in a constant situation of distrust and attacks on them, and have to win a 'daily majority' of their stakeholders' support, like any modern politician. That requires an ethical and political skill that many do not have: when to give in, and when to counter-attack, how to hedge a reputation but also how to build one. 'Reputation management' has become a key consultancy field and managerial task in international business. Reputation, as the saying goes, takes years to build and minutes to destroy.

If this be so, what's the environment like in which the executive finds him or herself? It is difficult enough to learn something about how the stakeholders now operate and how transnational press deals with alleged unethical businesses; about crisis management and proactive behaviour. But if I add to this burden by venturing to say that all this is made the more difficult today because of global insecurity, you may feel tempted to leave the room. Yet this is what's unfolding before our eyes: the much-praised globalization enhances the ethical void and makes it harder for the executive to know what ethics means and which standards to live up to. In a global world, he or she

---

[2]   *Financial Times*, 14 April 2004; feature by Michael Skapinker.

has to live and act both in a national and transnational context of expectations and demands.

Your HQ is in Stockholm, yet your manufacturing is in China. You are accused of exploiting workers by the Swedish press and your Swedish consumers organize a boycott of your products. Can you say that Chinese standards are different or do you have to stick to high Swedish standards? Is there a common human rights standard or not? Are you accountable to the Swedish stakeholders or to the whole world?

When I ran some cases about similar situations from Harvard Business School with the top management of a Norwegian firm, they expected me to provide the answers, and they also thought that there were set answers. One case was about differential treatment of indigenous oil workers and ex-pats on an Angolan rig. Can you treat these groups differently and respect human rights? Yes, in terms of wages and benefits, living quarters and holidays, was the general view; but no, not in terms of medical aid in case of accident or illness. My clients were very unsure of how to reason about human rights because they lacked the knowledge of how international norms are interpreted by the UN and other actors. They disliked the fact that there was no set answer. I told them that ethics is about *application* of general rules to real life situations; and the application is what they have to learn themselves; no one can coach them on this. When the crisis hits, they must know how to make the application. They must learn sound judgement before this happens. They must be able to stick to their judgement and defend it against stakeholders who may have a different point of view, or who may simply be malicious in seeking to bring them down.

Sound judgement is the key to it all, both to life in general and to the professional role. It used to be so simple: most of us were brought up in a generally Christian environment in Europe – some in a Jewish one – but all in all we shared the same Judaeo-Christian ethics. The Ten Commandments were known. They inspired our legislation about crime, sex, and business. This legislation was made inside each nation-state, and most business was firmly anchored inside it. Now the nation-state recedes while secularization reaches new lows, and the only ethical anchor remaining is international human rights.

Ethical insecurity now is directly linked to the break-down of the nation-state and the as yet unformed norms of international behaviour. As long as your business remained in Sweden, there were very clear norms of what politicians do, of what you should do, of workers' rights, etc. It was predictable and it was safe. Now political governance is weak or absent in the global market place while stakeholders are much more alert and targeted than before. NGOs with expert knowledge of one human right – e.g. child labour – will systematically scrutinize your business. If Amnesty International or Human Rights Watch accuses you, you are in terrible trouble even if the allegations may be unfounded.

A Norwegian case comes to mind: Telenor, the telecom-munications company, was accused by Amnesty of racist policies in Malaysia because it did not object to the national Malayan ethnic 'quota' system. Telenor's management was on the defensive, clearly not able to reply because it had not prepared for this eventuality. Amnesty's case was poor, and neither the Norwegian government nor the UN had criticized Malaysia. The Telenor reply in the press came more than a week late. The damage was done, on a groundless charge. The press had carried a series of articles on the topic before the CEO's rather timid response.

The lesson is clear. Be prepared, have a crisis manage-ment plan, but more than that: know your human rights and international politics. You should know what the UN says about a given country, and how international human rights standards are interpreted by the UN itself. The UN is the only legitimate body in these matters; it is no longer your nation-state. What the Swedish government thinks does not much matter in the global market place.

But beyond this – the obvious bottom line – there is a much more important issue that only a *kjernekar* can deal with, viz. having that sound judgement based on that inner core. How can one acquire this in the current situation? There are certainly no quick fixes here. But it is possible. I return to this in my conclusion.

Let me first address the physical and political risk of today's international system; and then the ethical risk entailed by this.

Physical and Political Risk under Globalization

Business leaders face physical insecurities as the nation-state recedes in importance and no global political regime replaces it. Doing business in so-called failed states entails great risk, ethically as well as physically. In Western democracies neo-liberalism erodes the state's monopoly on the legitimate use of violence, and privatized security and defence increases[3] as new threats abound, especially terrorism. Business leaders must cope on their own and decide how to hedge and protect their firm. They cannot rely on the nation-state to protect them in many regions. It is either not functioning, or as in Europe, loses political importance.

This much praised globalization process implies that the framework of the nation-state decreases radically in importance. This process, revolutionary as much as the formation of the nation-state also was, is not yet seen in its enormous ramifications.

Whereas failed states entail problems of chaos and great uncertainty, in EU-Europe we can meaningfully speak of the post-national phase. The nation-state has formed the limits of most human activity in terms of work and politics from the time of the treaties of Westphalia in 1648, where the principle of state sovereignty was laid down. In the Thirty Years War, which was ended by these treaties,

---

3   The best analysis of privatization of security is found in C. W. Singer's *Corporate Warriors: The Privatization of Defence*, Cornell University Press, Ithaca, 2003.

Europe experienced tremendous insecurity and chaos with non-state actors of all sorts equipping their own soldiers.

This is a situation similar to the failed state concept today, where statehood exists in name only in large parts of the world. In Africa, Central Asia, the Caucasus, and the Balkans there are no classical Weberian[4] states, and not only physical insecurity, but also ethical insecurity, meets the investor. *It is no coincidence that corruption abounds where the state does not exercise physical power.* No rule of law can exist where this primary condition is not met. Also in areas with so-called 'rogue states' or dictatorships, the problem of corruption is rampant. The Middle East comes to mind at once.

The problem of how to avoid corruption is on the top of the business executive's agenda these days.

There is a clear and logical link between rule of law, human rights, democracy – the investment climate business needs and craves – and the effective physical exercise of power. In failed states, there is neither, and the business leader courts a risky life indeed: is it possible to avoid bribes and kick-backs? Can you get an oil exploration licence without a major signature bonus? When does the bonus become a bribe?

While press and NGOs now scrutinize business in both failed and rogue state areas, business leaders cannot look the other way as has been the custom for many years. For instance, bribes in these areas used to be tax deductible in Norway until a few years ago; now it is a crime under Norwegian law after changes made in 2003. There is also a strong development of an international norm in this area:

---

[4]   Max Weber is known for the *locus classicus* in the definition of the state as the political entity with the monopoly on the legitimate use of force in a given territory. This was also the principle of Westphalia: sovereignty meant non-intervention; the ruler was in charge inside his territory. The concept of human rights is the very opposite logic of the state logic: human rights take precedence over sovereignty and borders.

the OECD has had a long-standing convention against the bribery of civil servants, but more importantly, highly respected NGOs like Peter Eigen's Transparency International are in the forefront of developing a norm of zero tolerance. This means that the standard in 'soft law' terms that one will be held accountable to, is this strong norm. Also of great importance here is the UN Global Compact initiated by Kofi Annan at the Davos World Economic Forum in 1999.

Thus, in the area of corruption a strong international norm is developing which enables stakeholders to demand compliance although this is not strictly legally binding (yet). The business leader accused of corruption really has no choice but to comply. This is extremely diffi-cult, as anyone with business experience in any of the geographical areas mentioned knows. But international legitimacy is an extremely powerful force: Norwegian state oil company Statoil recently saw both CEO and chair-man of the board leave on account of money transferred to an Iranian consultancy – money that seemed very exces-sive for the services rendered in terms of man hours. The normative pressure wielded through the press campaign was decisive: there was sufficient evidence of distrust in the management. Without trust there is loss of reputation and loss of shareholder value. In less tangible sectors – oil is after all only oil, and you need it regardless of the seller – but where brand really matters, this truth is even more important: if shareholder value is made up 80% of reputa-tion, who can live with a 'tainted' CEO?

In the case of corruption, managers have to be alerted to the international norm formation that goes on. The same holds for other issues, such as women's rights, child labour, fair pay, social responsibility, etc. In all these cases it is not the host country's norms that matter; it is the inter-national stakeholders' judgement. The executive may desperately want to reach out to political principals and ask: *What is the right thing to do? Is this a breach of human rights?* But who is to provide the answer in a global setting?

In the failed or rogue state, there is none to trust with an answer. The failed state is ungoverned in the sense of international legitimacy, and any political master's answer is bound to be worthless. In rogue states, local norms of human rights are naturally utterly wrong. In these kinds of states the international company executive has to make up his or her own mind about whether to invest and on the limits of engagement. There used to be a time when one could ask one's own government about the right course. Many a Norwegian executive thought that all that was necessary as far as human rights and international politics were concerned was to ask the Norwegian Foreign Office whether the country in question was under UN embargo: no embargo, no problem. This naive approach is wrong for two reasons: Norway the nation-state no longer counts in this regard; only the UN and the so-called 'international community' do; and a UN embargo is such a rare occurrence that only a handful of trouble spots experience it. There is no guidance in the old reflex to leave political problems to nominal national politicians.

The business executive is almost on his own. The national framework gone, he is faced with the double demand of knowing how to apply human rights and how to assess a concrete political situation. He also knows that there are new stakeholders, who operate transnationally, that monitor him: they go by the evolving human rights norms that are centered in the UN system. The key words in all this are human rights. One cannot be seen to violate human rights.

Yet a related difficulty is the rise of the cultural and political conflict between radical Islam and the perceived 'Western' norms of human rights and democracy. While we claim that these norms are universal, they are rejected as such by many cultures and states of the world. This tenuous situation makes the ethical wager harder for the business executive.

Ethical Risk Under Globalization

Although they are the only ethical norms in the global world, it is not easy to 'talk the talk' and 'walk the walk' of human rights. 'Talking the talk' is easy, but the rhetorical entrapment is instant: when a company makes human rights its cornerstone of branding, as, for example Shell has done, one has to follow up. Can the follow up ever be sufficient to satisfy the stakeholders?

By now all companies know that they must report along the triple bottom line, and the criteria for environmental reporting are getting more and more specific. The social responsibility bottom line is the newest and least specific: what should it mean?

The interesting observation I make from the position of international politics is that business leaders are more than often too naive and timid about these questions. They are naive if they think that every role that NGOs or politicians try to make them assume in this field is a sound one. They are timid when they let themselves be pushed into new social and sometimes political roles that business proper should not have.

There should be no 'beauty contest' about which companies assume the maximum human rights work. Companies should not assume political responsibilities, even in failed states. There are good social projects that one can aid in undertaking, but one should never do the job which is the duty of a government. An oil company in Africa was asked for the usual bribes for the import of their goods at the local airport. No, they said, we do not do this, but we can provide the airport with an air conditioning system. But next the government may want bridges and schools from them. What to do?

These are real dilemmas in failed state regions, and there is no easy answer. One good solution may be partnership through UN agencies or NGOs which assume the formal responsibility. We see this increasingly in developing countries.

Yet the key problem remains: which role is proper to

business in promoting human rights and democracy? Here the norms are forming and changing in the international setting right now, but there are relatively few business leaders who see that this is the window of opportunity for them to participate in this debate. The stakeholders here then are the UN and its Global Compact, the NGO community in the field, the various human rights stakeholders, some international press, and a good number of academics. This kind of informal process also takes place in other business sectors. Leaders who do not want to have norms imposed on them should now do much more to influence what these norms will be.

The ethical risk today is thus also an ethical opportunity: market actors have much more power than political governance systems at the international level. From my point of view this is sad and problematic, as politics concerns the 'common good' and must be above 'private' actors, like companies. Yet the short and brutal conclusion is that as the nation-state recedes, international politics does not replace it. Only the EU can aspire to be an effective governance system. The rest of international organizations are weak and sectorial.

This makes it tempting to make business play political roles, as I have warned against above. It also makes it incumbent upon business leaders to define their proper CSR role. There will be stakeholder pressure of various sorts: NGOs in the human rights field which want the market actors to play UN, press which charges your company with human rights abuses – sometimes rightly – and a discrepancy between the human rights standards of your home country and your host country.

With the demise of the national framework of doing business a lot of traditional norms of ethical behaviour have disappeared. But there is also the added and new 'problem' of transnational ethics – how to be consistent in both home and host country. The standards of human rights are one and uniform – they are in fact well defined for most human rights in both 'soft law' and in legally binding instruments. But the executive is left with the task of defining the proper application of these standards to individual cases. This is difficult unless one has knowledge of how human rights is usually justified in specific cases. I think it demands a very mature sense of ethics, something to which I return below.

The ethical risk to which the global firm is exposed consists of the lack of clear guidelines for ethical application beyond the individual nation-state, but also in the new expectations put on firms for not only behaving ethically, but for promoting human rights and CSR; to be active proponents of doing good. This idea is a good and noble one, as market actors wield tremendous power in many places; but it is also risky for the firm. The question of exactly which role the firm should have in this presents itself at once, and none but the business leader can provide the answer. Yet many stakeholders will have differing views, so the leader has to be able to argue for and defend his choice in this regard. If he opts for doing business in Myanmar, he must count on widespread attacks, but perhaps his position is the right one if his business actually contributes to helping certain groups. For the time being the international jury judges against this; but there are many other examples where there is real doubt. As a rule of thumb it makes ethical sense to be in almost any country – this is both a political and a business truth.

The stakeholders that make up the company environment are of various types and have their own interests. I think it is essential to recognize this. Too often one naively thinks that an NGO promotes the morally good per se. But NGOs also have their institutional interests. Consumers today are sometimes called citizens with consumer power. Not having any direct international influence, they can acquire consumer power more easily than political power. They are a considerable force to be reckoned with. The press is the omnipresent force that is ignored at one's peril. Learning how the press works is essential. If there are skeletons in your closet, they will be found.

In conclusion, there is much more ethical insecurity in

the global marketplace than in the nation-state era. Increased physical and political insecurity also contributes to this.

Conclusion: The Ethical Core

Do ethics really matter when power is in play? Yes, they do, and increasingly so. The best recent example is the almost total loss of moral standing that the Bush administration now experiences. A war declared from the moral high ground of the superior political system and culture, for 'freedom and democracy' has become a fiasco. The loss of US credibility in the world is enormous.

First, there was a disregard for the common UN norm of obtaining a Security Council mandate. This 'sin' might have been forgiven in the court of world public opinion if the war had truly liberated the oppressed or disclosed real threats of Weapons of Mass Destruction (WMDs). In both those cases a common sense of justice would have been supportive, even though no state will ever declare that the UN should be disregarded.

But as no WMDs were found and the case for 'regime change' was tainted by indigenous opposition to the liberators, the moral case for war was weakened. The invasion was a showpiece of modern war, but the post-conflict phase was incompetently handled. But the real blow to US credibility of course came with the disclosure of the treatment of prisoners of war.

The essence here is reputation and credibility – the morals of the situation. Here also trust enters. The more chaotic and insecure the environment, the more trust is required. When I was a deputy foreign minister, a common theme was always – as in business negotiations – 'can we trust them to keep their word?'

This trust cannot be learnt; it is a reflection of the behaviour over time of a person or a company, or even a state. If you advertise your mission in the world as one of liberating the oppressed to bring them the morally superior political system of democracy, human rights and the rule of law, you cannot behave like an outlaw.

There are many lesser cases where the process is the same. The press drives a process and ultimately the leader has to resign, with much damage being done to the company's reputation.

In these situations the ethical 'core' that I introduced initially is indispensable. The leader has to be able to react correctly in a very tense, stressful and risky situation. A golden rule with the press is that whatever you say must be true. The 'no comment' is always bad. The press works in a sequence: the first article about your company is never the last. When the journalist calls you to have your comment on it – often late the night before printing – he is simply initiating the 'confrontation phase'. This is an awful situation for any leader. The initiative lies with the press; the journalist has done his research; the paper is ready for a long offensive if necessary, usually with the aim of bringing you and the company down. Many times the press simply does its job, but the logic of the press is always unpleasant for the 'victim' – it is a specific angle, a framing of the issue that has to have news value.

The good leader in this nightmarish situation is one who is prepared, who knows the skeletons in the closet if there are any; who has thought through this kind of campaign, and who knows what to say. The very best leaders manage to take an offensive stand, sometimes by calling their own press conference and offering the whole story. This requires both the ability to take risk and to have audacity in the eye of the storm; but also the prudence to consider the issues that may be critical long beforehand. Crisis management is not enough.

The words I have used in the above paragraph – audacity, prudence, courage – are what are known as virtues.

The solution to finding the ethical core lies here. There is a tradition from classical European thought that should be rediscovered. It is the knowledge about human nature, about its so-called virtues and vices. The Greeks and the Romans developed this essential knowledge about how to become properly ethical to the fullest, and Christianity built on the human virtues, adding the supernatural ones of faith, hope, and charity.

To the post-modern mind, the concept of human nature sounds oddly essentialist. Yet human nature exists, and is a constant. As the Greek philosophers very well knew, a person can become strong, wise, good, courageous – or descend into being a brute – weak, imprudent, cowardly, slothful, lazy, even evil. This choice is yours. If you opt for the virtues, you must acquire knowledge about yourself and train yourself, not only physically, but morally. *Askesis* is a Greek word that means training.

The Romans were interested in how to be strong and courageous in tough times, not unlike our own. They developed stoicism, a philosophy of such inner strength. The Christians naturally emphasized the redeemed nature of man, pointing out that our vocation is to do good in a measure far beyond our seeming strength.

Today this knowledge about human nature and its ability for training in virtues is largely forgotten. Yet it was the staple education for any schoolboy in Europe for more than 2000 years. It has often surprised me that business leaders are so naive about human nature, especially their own. How often have we seen leaders – in both business and politics – who have fallen because of greed? Of lust? Of a senseless egoism? In innumerable cases. The vices tend to dominate where virtue is not developed.

Chapter Five

On 'Politicized' Law and 'Juridified' Politics in Europe

In a very rich and suggestive paper, 'The Idea of Human Dignity as the Center of Modern Constitutional States', presented at the Pontifical Academy of Social Science, Vatican City, 18–22 November 2005, Professor Kirchhof provides a very interesting *Ideengeschichte* about European legal philosophy and meta-legal concepts, and the author makes it very clear that the concept of human dignity has a specific, objective meaning. This dignity, which is the basis on which rights are founded, is above the law and pre-existing to it. This, for example, is expressed in the preamble to the Universal Declaration, which expressly states that the rights therein are 'inherent' and 'inalienable' because they are founded on human dignity.

Kirchhof notes that all declarations about rights contain preambles that 'provide warranty that human dignity, as a predetermined starting point, is at the same time a legal axiom of a constitutional concept. Ultimately, this concept cannot be proven or refuted.'[1]

He further notes how the suppressed have used the 'rights' concept to argue for freedom and political entitlement, and that human dignity has been the universal

---

[1]   Kirchhof, pp. 3–4.

starting point for this: rights based on dignity are not Englishmen's rights, as the Americans argued, and prior to this, they were not the rights of the lords, but of all free men in Magna Carta.

The paper then moves on to discuss the impact of Christian anthropology on European law. Dignity to the ancient Greeks and to the Romans, argues Kirchhof, was equal to fame, reputation, and honour: 'The ancient Greeks had no general conception of dignity'.[2] Here I would venture to object: Socrates, as we know him through the Platonic dialogues, certainly speaks about a common human dignity which enables the person to become virtuous – he or she can choose between virtues and vices, and has a free choice. This anthropology is very similar to the Christian one – free will, striving for human virtue, *askesis* to that end, etc. The Christian 'additions' to this are the so-called cardinal virtues of 'faith, hope and charity'. But the dignity that Plato presents is far from outwardly or superficial – Socrates takes the hemlock precisely because he is a just man who does not compromise for personal advantage. In Aristotle's *Politics* we find the same view of the just and noble man, evident in the classification criteria of good and bad regimes. The Roman law makers also have a concept of *dignitas* in the Stoa, as Kirchhof remarks.

The contribution of Christianity to the concept of human dignity is connected with the novelty in this religion that man is created in the image of God, which implies a radical equality. The doctrine of redemption also implies that the weak and the 'non-performers' in terms of virtue share in the very same dignity as the rest, and that the weak and sick are God's special 'children'. Charity regardless of 'deservedness' is the new element. Law also becomes universal through Christianity – there is 'neither Greek nor Jew'. But from the very beginning of political philosophy the city of God and the city of man are separated – politics and law have their own autonomy, and the

[2] Ibid., p. 6.

state is separate from religion. The gods of the state were the state's own in ancient times; no longer so.

Empirically this influence can be traced; take the 'hard' case of my own country, where the pagan Viking king Olav Haraldsson became a Christian (c.1012–15) and later introduced Christianity as the state's religion in Norway. The legal system, well developed by the Vikings, was changed in terms of marriage laws, laws about *utbur* – the abandonment of sick children to die in the woods, and in terms of the same procedure for the old and sick. Human and animal sacrifices were outlawed, and the legal changes were so substantial that the legal system was renamed *Kristen-retten* (the Christian Law). As the sagas of Snorre Sturlason relate, these changes were so unpopular that they had to be enforced by might.[3]

There is no doubt, then, about the empirical influence of both Roman law and Christian concepts on European jurisprudence, but the problem today which Kirchhof goes on to address after his historical exposé, is that *human dignity and human rights today mean a variety of things to a variety of people*. There is no agreement on how to define these concepts.

I remember discussing the concept of human dignity with Norwegian radical feminists prior to the Women's Conference in Beijing in 1995. They wanted to delete the concept from the concluding text, thinking that it meant some kind of *bourgeois* complacency for women – 'you can get dignity and sit at home and be nobly quiet'. I pointed out that the concept is a standard one in all human rights documents, and then they said: 'What does it mean?' Well, that is not easy to explain; it is a little like the term 'cultivated': we recognize someone as a culti-vated person, but it is not easy to put in words when perhaps the other person does not know what it already

3   J. Haaland Matláry, 'Restaurer les racines chretiennes de la politique européenne', *Sedes sapientiæ*, 90., Societe Saint-Thomas-D'Aquin, Chemere-le-Roi, December 2004, pp. 77–99.

means. The Norwegian feminists had a point: what in fact does it mean in a culture that is radically pluralist and certainly post-Christian? And is it important in today's politicization of human rights when they are redefined anyway?

Politics and Law: Variations on a Theme

Kirchhof spends the latter part of his paper in a critique of modern Western anthropology, and he is undoubtedly right in pointing out that there are strong tendencies of greed, egoism, decadence, etc. at hand. In terms of respect for life, the latest development in the direction of euthanasia as a 'human right' is disturbing indeed. But it does not do to invoke legal definitions to answer the questions posed – of which there are many in the paper. If human dignity is nothing and everything to most people, it is because there is no experience of human nature and the human condition that is common to all any more. Kirchhof asserts that 'In a constitutional system characterized by the idea that man is endowed with dignity, the majority will never oppress the minority. The democratic development of man's will continually respects the pre-existing, and for this reason legally pre-determined, dignity of each person.'[4] This quotation betrays wishful thinking rather than reality. The current reality is that even lawyers state that human rights instruments are 'political statements', as Norwegian Constitutional Court Judge Karen Bruzelius said at a recent seminar.[5] The 'legal method' for their interpretation is called 'the dynamic method' which essentially means that political changes in the definition of human rights will be reflected in the case law of the courts, be

---

[4]   Ibid., p. 23.
[5]   'Intervention', Conference on Legal Intergration in Europe, 16–17 September 2005, Faculty of Law, Oslo University.

it in Strasbourg or Luxembourg, Oslo or Karlsruhe. Bruzelius, herself a lawyer, hastens to add that 'we judges do not do policy-making'. But this is dangerously close to a semantic exercise.

Kirchhof laments the 'decline' in human standards, if we can call them that, and the implications this has for the *Rechtsstaat*. However, he ends where the analysis becomes very interesting, viz. in the present period. There is in fact a logic at work in the relationship between human rights and democracy: if we opt for total freedom to define and redefine human rights, we undermine the very concept of human rights, and also the idea of a *Rechtsstaat* because parliamentary majority will decide everything. There will be nothing left for the constitutional court to stand on, as it were – judicial review becomes impossible. The *Rechtsstaat* presupposes that human rights can be defined objectively or at least that there is a distinctly legal way of reviewing redefinitions of them. It is clear that human rights 'evolve' with time – new rights are discovered that were not in the original declaration, but these cannot contradict the fundamental human rights. What is law and what is politics in this highly important 'cocktail' is deeply contested, but my point is simply that the logical connection between upholding human rights and democracy at the same time – in fact, upholding the *Rechtsstaat* – presupposes that human rights are not products of the ongoing political process, but that they are objective standards against which political majority decisions may be tested. Human rights are to act as the guarantee of fundamental rights for the person against state power, not as the instrument of the state against the citizen.

Human rights, emanating from the concept of human dignity, are today what we call 'essentially contested' in all Western states. The law in most of them follows the evolution of politics, even if there are states like Germany where the power of the constitutional court is great. The strongest *Rechtsstaat*-tradition in Europe is found in Germany precisely because of the experience of democratic politics 'gone wild' in the Hitler years. But this court–politics balance is also a political choice in the end.

There is no recipe for the 'best of all possible worlds', to paraphrase Voltaire. In the US judges are elected, not named; and the Supreme Court decides the value questions that are the most controversial in the polity. Most Europeans would say that this system represents a severe degree of politicization of law, and we find the idea of an elected judge highly improper, a 'misalliance' between politics and law. How can the political impartiality of judges be upheld in such a system?

My point is that the law and legal system always reflects the religious, political, and cultural setting of a given polity. This is complicated enough, but today the law is increasingly supra-national; the paradox is really in the Bruzelius quotation above: judges, often in supra-national courts, adjudicate in human rights cases based on more or less political trends, but nominally present them as law – they *become* law by virtue of this procedure – and these cases are then transposed into national law, setting precedents legally and politically. Most European states, regardless of whether they have a monist or dualist system, accept the European Court of Human Rights (ECHR) and the European Court of Justice (ECJ) (now also adjudicating in human rights cases to an increasing extent in connection with the large internal market portfolio) as law that is above their own. The irony is that this law may be a largely political product that is not only made by judges, but also by foreign judges.

Supra-National Juridification: Double Democratic Deficit?

In my institute we directed and conducted a five-year study (1997–2002) entitled *Maktutredningen* (the Norwegian Power Study)[6] assigned by the government,

---

[6] NOU (Norwegian Public Investigations) 1999:19, 'Domstolene i samfunnet', Ø. Østerud, F. Engelstad and P. Selle, i Makten og Demokratiet: En sluttbok fra Makt- og Demokratiutredningen, Oslo, 2003.

investigating who has which kind of power in society. We found ample evidence of the trend towards 'juridification' of politics and also that this took place internationally to a growing extent. Human rights is the name of the game for all politics these days, and entails an almost complete relativism in changing human rights. Kirchhof's hope that there can be one understanding of human dignity and specific human rights is therefore not likely to be fulfilled. The problem is rather that there is a pluralist view – an essential contestation – of all these rights.

Specifically, we found that Norwegians use the concept of human rights in a general sense in order to promote their political claims; not referring to any specific human right in any specific convention or declaration, but rather in the sense of a 'good thing' – it is my human right and it is my dignity that demands this – here we also have the concept of human dignity invoked in the political discourse. Increasingly this concept is used to justify ever new claims to new rights, such as rights to more pension, work, more parental leave when a child is born, better medical treatment for the handicapped, the elderly, the sick in general, improved conditions for women, improved rights for children – 'it is undignified for them to have to labour with homework when adults can decide on how to spend their off-work hours', etc. Undoubtedly many of these claims are really questions of dignity – can there ever be good enough care for the sick and old? If we accept that equality is the basic democratic norm, the answer is that human dignity is only fulfilled when all citizens have top quality health care all their lives, regardless of income and social status. Thus, we cannot easily dismiss the everyday usage of the terms human dignity and human rights for pressing issues politically. Everyone agrees on the importance of human rights – again undoubtedly a good thing – and it is also true that they can almost always be improved upon. The medical care given to old people, as an example, was much worse before than now, when medical improvements are enormous. The issue is where to say stop, not that there are valid claims based on human dignity.

Secondly, we found that Norwegians increasingly invoke specific legal claims to human rights under the ECHR when they disagree with Norwegian authorities or courts. Several times over the years the Norwegian state has been sentenced in the Strasbourg court and has complied each time, changing national legislation. Now citizens are familiar with the convention and the court, and use the threat of bringing a case to Strasbourg as leverage in the political processes. They can concern issues such as the mandatory teaching of Christianity in public schools – is it a contravention of the human right to religious freedom? Or the state church, a violation of the same right? What about the right to medical treatment outside the state if such treatment is not possible in Norway? The threat of using the court system, including the national courts, is growing in importance. The usual process is one in which the media portray a case of for example, alleged discrimination – a state church pastor is denied a job because he lives with a homosexual partner, which is allowed in the 'partnership law' – can the state force the state church to accept this or not?   The Norwegian state then has to calibrate its standpoints to international human rights standards, anticipating the outcome of a prospective court ruling, and argue in human rights terms. The whole political process becomes 'juridified' as well as 'internationalized'.

The method used by the Court is called 'the dynamic method'. This method of interpretation is described by former court president Rudolf Bernhardt as 'evolutive interpretation' and by Matthijs de Blois as 'sociological method'. This is further defined as a widening of human rights, not as a restriction. Emberland notes that the court takes the view that stronger human protection is its mission, and this is a teleological or evolutive view of human rights.

But how can the Court legitimate this principle which has not been imposed on it and which is not part of the convention itself? There is no answer to this question. When we further ask how the principle is interpreted, we get the answer that it is largely a question of how politics in Europe evolves: law follows political trends. This is partially legitimated as a function of international law, which always evolves, but also with reference to a rather vague idea about political change in European states: 'Sometimes the Court – without documentation – will put emphasis on changes in the climate of opinion in signatory states to the Convention'.[7] Emberland finds this particularly disconcerting, as the Court invokes political trend changes but does not document them: where they take place, they should be heeded. I would add that the principle itself is a major problem from the legal point of view, for how can human rights be anything but 'politics with a time lag' when the most important human rights court in the world deems human rights to be equal in content to political trends?

Another source of supra-national legislation in the human rights field is the ECJ in Luxembourg. As ECJ judge and scholar Allan Rosas, professors Hjalte Rasmussen and Joseph Weiler have shown,[8] this court not only engages strongly in judicial activism which is also teleological, as the court is treaty-bound to aim at integration ('an ever closer union'), but it also sentences more and more human rights cases. Rosas documents how the court started to refer to the ECHR and to human rights as early as 1969 when it referred to 'the fundamental human rights enshrined in the general principles of Community law and protected by the court' and stated that these belong to the basis on which the court adjudicates.[9] Throughout the

---

[7] Ibid., p. 7.
[8] Hjalte Rasmussen, *On Law and Policy in the European Court of Justice*, Dorcrecht, Boston, 1986, and Joseph Weiler, *The Constitution of Europe*, Cambridge University Press, Cambridge, 1999.
[9] Case 29/69 *Stauder vs City of Ulm*-ECR 419 and case 11/70 *Internationale Handelsgesellschaft*-ECR 1125.

years the ECJ has expanded greatly in its human rights 'portfolio', interpreting its mandate in internal market treaty rules as also a matter of human rights. For instance, an affirmative action policy proposed by the University of Oslo in order to increase the number of female professors by instituting professorships for women only, was struck down by the ECJ as discriminatory of men, and was therefore abandoned.[10]

The relevance of these two examples to our theme is the following: European states are developing more and more of a supra-national court system for the adjudication of human rights. As these rights are universal, this is a positive development, as the problem is often that human rights are not enforced and therefore have no teeth. But there are also problems with this development: if judges are more policy-makers than they like to admit, we have a system of supra-national and unelected policy-makers that define our human rights standards.

Returning to the Bruzelius quote, she said that 'human rights paragraphs are really policy statements', meaning that there are few indications of how a lawyer should interpret them.[11] Even if one uses a positivist definition of law and says that 'law is what lawyers do', there is a problem of legal method here. Norwegian lawyers are in fact very worried about the internationalization trend for this very reason: which legal sources and methods should they employ? Professor Hans-Petter Graver characterizes the present situation as one of 'liquid law':

> The main argument ... is that in a situation where legislators, judges and subjects of the law have to cope with a law

---

[10] Norway is not in the EU, but is bound by ECJ adjudication through an agreement with the EU which obliges Norway to accept all EU directives and which has its own intermediate court. In practice, the ECJ decides.

[11] Intervention at the conference 'European Legal Intergration: Contemporary Challenges', Faculty of Law, University of Oslo, 16 and 17 September, 2005.

that is increasingly polycentric, with an abundance of sources and higher degree of instability and change than within the traditional national legal order, no fixed points of reference exist for drawing lines between 'activism' and 'restraints' in judicial decision-making.[12]

He adds that Robert Bork's[13] argument that judges globally engage in judicial activism now seems borne out by the trends in Europe, and points out that the terms have several meanings (and that none of them is an agreed-upon definition). His concern is mainly that Norwegian judges, accustomed to a pragmatic view of law which is very faithful to precedent and national sources, are now introduced to a pluralist setting in Europe where the questions of method and legislating from the bench are wide open: 'Failure to use the established "tools of the trade" is another form of "judicial activism"'[14] and this happens because 'Norwegian courts are forced to engage in a formalist approach based on foreign rules and legal principles'.[15]

This situation eventually leads to a blurring of legality and politics, of what is legal and what is political. Graver's disconcerting conclusion is worth quoting in full, the more so because it comes from an eminent expert on EU law:

Maybe the relations between different legislators and courts in the European legal order may be described by the metaphor 'liquid law' where the law is fluent, unable to hold its shape for long, undergoing a continuous change in shape when subjected to stress. Legal rules based on national legislation will prevail for a time, but change when subjected to challenges from European law. Doctrines based on precedents are abandoned or adapted

---

[12]   H.-P. Graver, 'Community Law, Judicial Activism and Liquid Rules – an EEA Perspective', paper presented at the conference 'European Legal Intergration: Contemporary Challenges', op. cit.

[13]   R. Bork, *Coercing Virtue: The Worldwide View of Judges*, Washington D. C., 2003.

[14]   Graver, op. cit., p. 9.

[15]   Ibid., p. 10.

when subjected to pressures from other courts, political bodies or articulated social interests. Judges are increasingly emancipated from rules, codes, and practices and faced with conflicting demands from a polycentric web of legal authorities. *One can no longer distinguish sharply between the political function of legislation and the judicial function of interpretation and application* [my emphasis].[16]

The field where this is most evident is human rights. If we continue to use the Norwegian case as an example, the political process of 'judicialization' of human rights 'politics' is clearly a development in the American direction. Several other indicators of such a general change include the end of Keynesianism and the strong dominance of New Public Management ideology, whereby the citizen is seen more as a consumer, client and right-holder than as a citizen in a polity where what is political is well defined. With the end of the cold war, the nation-state in Europe has become less important, and empirically we find that 'human rights activism has proceeded after (this time), and during the 1990s the ECHR became incorporated as domestic law by most member states'.[17]

In the area of human rights, international courts have acquired sovereignty that is now much more important than before because citizens invoke the rights in a transnational manner. Østerud notes, very importantly, that 'the background to the strong lawmaking role of transnational courts is that there are no political lawmakers at the transnational level. International law, and indeed human rights, is developing from treaties with wide and imprecise clauses' (my emphasis).[18] Thus, we have a complex law-politics situation in Europe today.

Judges perform 'semi-politics' when they adjudicate in human rights, but they are not politicians. These judge-

---

[16]   Graver, op. cit., p. 20.
[17]   Ø. Østerud, 'Power, Judicialisation and Parliamentary Democracy', p. 6, paper presented at Stiftung Wissenschaft u. Politik, 2–4 June 2005.
[18]   Ibid., p. 11.

ments bind national courts: 'fluid' law is imposed on
nation-states. But politics also becomes 'juridified' when
citizens not only use the courts instead of the parliamentary channel, but insist on defining political issues as
human rights issues. This endangers the model of the
Rechsstaat from two sides, in a 'pincer-movement': from
above, in the imposition of 'fluid' law, and from below, in
the constant invocation of human rights in the political
process.

Moreover, we see that the drivers behind this development are global and probably irreversible. The discourse
on human rights is universal, and the West exports human
rights everywhere, as discussed below. The loss of political power inside the nation-state continues, as economic
globalization imposes a global logic on states. National
economic solutions are no longer possible. Likewise, the
citizen knows and compares what services the 'service-
state' created by New Public Management can provide: is
there a better cure for cancer in Australia? Then I demand
that my state pays for it. The scope of human rights
demands will only be determined by global possibilities
and one's own power. By creating binding international
human rights instruments, states have placed themselves
under the constant scrutiny of the newly empowered
global citizen, who will take his claims to the supra-
national level of adjudication if he has the resources to do
so.

The conclusion to this 'opening-up' or perhaps 'end of'
the nation-state is that human rights and human dignity
have moved to centre stage of world politics. This is no
small cause for celebration. But the concomitant development is that the *Rechtsstaat* at the national level cannot
function as the balancing mechanism between human
rights and majority politics any longer, and further, that
there is no consensus on what human dignity and human
rights mean. As we have seen, law and politics *are* already
very blurred, and that across the national–international
divide. Thus, Professor Kirchhof's regrets about the
dysfunctionality of the national system may be correct, but

they do not capture the complexity of the present situation in Europe, which spans the national-international divide as well as the law–politics distinction.

Is there any way out of this labyrinth? Let's assume that we want to ensure a functioning *Rechtsstaat* at the supranational level in some form or other – which I think is the only realistic way given the severe changes away from the nation-state – the most pressing question is not one of organization, i.e. of how national parliaments will still interact with such a court – but it is the question of agreement on fundamental norms. Is it possible to agree what human dignity and fundamental human rights mean in a post-modern, post-national, and post-Christian era? Is law 'liquid', as Professor Graver calls it, paraphrasing Zygmunt Baumann's concept of 'liquid modernity' where everything is 'individualized, privatized, without given or self-evident rules, codes and patterns to conform to'? [19]

The remainder of this chapter seeks to address this question.

To sum up: Europe has become the major exponent of human rights, democracy, and the rule of law all over the world. This modern 'trinity' of values has become the universal standard for good government and humane politics. While democracy entails a basic equality as the main norm, it is in human rights that we find today the values about the human being expressed in the form of so-called fundamental human rights. Rule of law means that there is a separation of powers with an independent judiciary. There can be no real democracy and rule of law unless it is based on human rights.

No one today questions the legitimacy of human rights as the basis for democracy; the procedure whereby the people decide. Rule of law ideally reflects the same human rights, and constrains the majority when it deviates from these standards. Human rights hang logically together with democracy and rule of law: these legal and political

---

[19]   Graver, op. cit., p. 20.

institutions cannot exist without the founding, which is a certain and very specific view of the human person – an anthropology. Conversely, human rights require democracy and rule of law – these rights are not respected under tyranny, oligarchy or any kind of one-party system.

Legal and Political Rationality: The Logic of Universals

Josef Cardinal Ratzinger wrote much on the problem of relativism versus pluralism. In his book *Werte in Zeiten des Umbruchs*[20] he states that while relativism is a precondition for democracy, there is nonetheless a fundamental difference between pluralism and nihilism:

> On the one hand there is the radical relativist position which denies the concept of the common good of the common weal (*summum bonum*) in politics because it is seen as metaphysical and then there is no other political principle than majority decision – against this position is the thesis that truth is not the product of politics, but is prior to politics and enlightens it. Politics practice does not create truth, but truth results from rationality; what we call natural law.[21]

The point of the second position is simply that the human being is able to use his reason to arrive at political and moral axioms; what we call justice in the tradition from Socrates onwards. Through reason and man's ability to evaluate arguments about right and wrong is the way to politics and law. To the ancients the difference was obvious; one could distinguish between a good ruler and a tyrant, between a usurper of power who uses it for his private interests, and a statesman. Whenever we use these

---

[20] Josef Cardinal Ratzinger, *Werte in Zeiten des Umbruchs*, Herder Bucherei, Freiburg, 2005.

[21] Ibid., p. 52. English translation provided by author.

distinctions, we automatically provide evidence of this moral sense that is inherent in the human being (but not in animals). Why, then, is it so hard to admit that politics is intimately connected to morals, and that human beings can reason about right and wrong in a fairly consistent manner? It seems that the opposite norm is the main one today; that of nihilism: there is only my view of things and your view of things, and no common objective standard other than in some few areas.

CHAPTER SIX

WHEN DEMOCRACY AND HUMAN RIGHTS COLLIDE: THE FAMILY AND FREEDOM OF RELIGION

The Family

There are broadly two classes of argument in the political debate about the family: those that rest on the presumption of constructivism – gender, not sex, is socially constructed, sex roles are thus constructed, and sex is constructed in terms of the feminine and the masculine and variations 'in between', more like a continuum than two categories. In turn this means that fatherhood and motherhood are socially constructed, and therefore the family can be freely defined and redefined. In fact, on this view it is pointless to seek a definition, as there is none to be found. What was the typical 'nuclear family' in some societies in some historical periods, changes. When the empirical manifestations of the family dissolve into many types of households, the definition of the family also changes. This argument is embedded in a view of society and politics that sees both as processes where there is no *Fester Punkt* to be discovered.

The other point of view, the natural law argument, assumes the existence of a fixed human nature, consisting of two sexes, where the family is a natural and constant institution in human life – it makes sense to speak of something as *natural*. Motherhood and fatherhood are therefore constants, and the family cannot be redefined, but exists as a norm in all societies, albeit with many instances that differ from the norm, due to widowhood, single parents, etc. The social roles of the sexes are however malleable and thus, 'socially constructed' to a great extent. Yet motherhood and fatherhood exist as 'archetypes' of human existence with much more than mere biological qualities.

Corresponding to these two views on the family's constituent units, the parents, we find two entirely different views on the rule of law *(Rechststaat)*, the status of international human rights, and the limits of politics. To the constructivist viewpoint corresponds the view that 'all is politics', as one critic put it to me: there are no limits to the political process in terms of human rights, and what we call human rights today, can be changed tomorrow, as we define new human rights. Likewise, if a majority today thinks that the traditional form of the family is obsolete, how can anyone stop it from redefining it when the ultimate political decision-making belongs on the national level, to the electorate in a given nation-state?

Similarly, the view of law that we usually call 'natural law' corresponds to the new that there is a human nature which can be discovered and defined; international human rights are apolitical and pre-political, resting on the discovery of human nature and its dignity. If the family is protected and privileged by human rights, they are valid in all places at all times. Given the turn of international politics after Nuremberg, whose famous trials laid down the validity of natural law above all positive law, this is a very strong argument. But as we know, to paraphrase Tip O'Neill, 'all politics is local': who can sanction a national parliament who passes a law that contravenes international human rights? Furthermore, to this view belongs the assumption that the public and the private are definable, that politics is limited to the issues of the common weal. In the case of the family this means that its political relevance lies in its childrearing: it needs protection from political intrusion but also political protection.

Thus, this chapter deals with the political battle over the definition of marriage and family which presently rages in the Western world. The strategic, concerted effort to redefine these institutions is the latest and most politically explicit in a long development that has weakened both. Marriage is rarer than ever before in the West, and families are also weaker because the birth rate is at an ebb in most European states. Other well-known factors are cohabitation as a literal *modus vivendi* that increasingly replaces marriage, high divorce rates and secularization which deducts the spiritual dimension from both marriage and family, reducing the union to the purely natural dimension.

However, it is only now that we face a campaign to actually redefine both marriage and family in terms of law. The reason why these arguments are partially so successful is that they reflect general notions of right and wrong in European public opinion. These general notions of what is reasonable and acceptable have evolved for many reasons, and it is very important to analyse these: how can it be explained that the words and concepts of motherhood, fatherhood and family seem reactionary, conservative and 'Christian' in our public debate? In short, what gives positive connotations and therefore political power to some concepts and not to others?

The answer to this question is crucial, because it also reflects on an underlying reality of philosophical and anthropological premises in people's minds.

In the end this implies that if the family is to be retained in Western politics in the form we know it so far, there has to be an understanding of its lived reality. There is no 'recognition' of what a mother is unless one has some observation and experience of a real mother, naturally in relation to her children. The same goes for fatherhood: what it really is can only be known through lived experience which precedes legal, philosophical and theological explanations of the phenomenon of fatherhood.

I want to insist on the crucial importance of this point: it has often struck me that these concepts are hardly fully known in my own country any more, and we often say that 'marriage' and 'family' are extremely weak institutions here. Empirically this is true; as cohabitation takes over more and more, and as there is no teaching on the Christian meaning of these institutions from the state church, which is the predominant one. This church is remarkably silent on the topic. When the traditional family structure disappears more and more from society, people no longer know what we talk about. This is a simple, but dramatic point: when I am in so-called 'Catholic' societies, I sometimes encounter 'strong' families and it strikes me that this is a 'real family', this is what family really means. It has everything to do with a deep naturalness that is integrated, of course, with the spiritual meaning of family, fatherhood and motherhood and their natural unity with the children. One could say that the Catholic teaching on the family is shown in practice: the *natural* unit acquires a *supernatural* dimension in those families, a quality and reality which is recognizable if not tangible.

The seriousness of this point cannot be overstated: the implication is that if family life as we have known it historically disappears, we cannot sustain the concepts much longer after that. This is the situation in which we find ourselves in Scandinavia: when family life *de facto* means all sorts of combinations of households, who can argue that there is a norm? Today more than 50% of Norwegian children are born out of wedlock, and this then, statistically, has become the norm. Given a positivist view of law, the law must reflect the reality of social practice and majority will. Family based on marriage is no longer the norm in that sense, but family based on cohabitation.

The National Level: Redefining Marriage in Norway

Some time ago I wrote the article below in my column in the Norwegian daily paper *Vårt Land*:

Why is the family politically relevant?

The family consists of mother, father, and children. It is a natural institution in all societies and society is obliged to support it because it uniquely brings forth and rears children. Mother and children have a right to special political support because a pregnant or nursing mother is vulnerable yet provides the most important work in any society. The family is politically relevant because it is here humans are born and raised: parents do the key work for society, and no one can replace them. It is in fact the basic cell of society.

These are not my words. They are a synopsis of the contents of the UN Declaration of Human Rights of 1948, the authoritative document in international law about human rights; source of all subsequent such documents.

These human rights are not a political construct, but have human dignity as their basis. They cannot be changed by political will or majorities; they are so-called <u>natural law</u>*, pre-political and apolitical. They supercede national laws.*

In modern times it was the <u>Nuremberg</u> *process against the Nazis that stated the natural law principle as the basis of human rights: there are laws above the positive law of states, and one is in fact bound to disobey this positive law if it contradicts natural law. The Nazis in Nuremberg were sentenced to death because they did not follow natural law, but German positive law in the genocide on Jews. After Nuremberg it was decided that human rights must be stated in a solemn declaration binding on all states so that it is clear that a higher law stands above political processes in individual states.*

The definition and rights of the family are such natural laws. Should Norway enact laws that change this, Norway would be in material breach of international human rights; an extremely serious matter.

Children have a right to know and live with their biological parents

Children have the right to know and live with their biological parents, and if this is not possible, they have a right to adoptive parents who resemble the natural parents as much as possible;

i.e. a mother and father. Further, the best interest of the child shall govern all issues relating to children's rights; and never the interest of adults. All children have a mother and a father, even if the sexual act is replaced by some insemination technique.

Again, these are not my words, but a synopsis of the contents of the UN Convention on the Rights of the Child from 1989. This legally binding convention leaves no doubt about the right of the child to his or her parents; not only to know them but also to be raised by them. This is what is meant by the 'best interest of the child'. <u>This implies that it is an injustice to conceive a child with the intention of raising it alone or in a homosexual relationship.</u> Even if adults desire children, this natural inclination goes against the best interest of the child in such cases.

If the family loses its privileged political support, society will be eroded from within. There must be no confusion about what a family is, and about children's rights. The document is extremely clear and realistic, necessary now because several Western states have started to redefine the family and dilute its importance in the process. At issue is the very core of human rights themselves: we cannot let minority interest groups undermine these. It is obvious to most that even if a majority reintroduced slavery, it would go against the natural law of human dignity – slavery is forbidden because it violates basic human rights. It should be equally obvious that no political minority or majority can change the rights of the most vulnerable in our society; viz. the children.

(Translated from the Norwegian)

One set of reactions to this article was astonishment at the idea that something in politics or law could be stated as an objective fact; in other words that human rights are apolitical. The natural law argument is clearly extremely unacceptable. I will seek to explain this.

The objection about the presumption of natural law in my human rights argument was common: that there is something that is objectively defined; something apolitical and pre-political. One critic thought that this was very naive; as 'everyone knows that everything is politics';

another thought I used a domination technique in stating that human rights are objectively defined and not given by politicians.

Here we are at the very core of the conceptual premises, of the meta-level of politics: the ideological assumptions of natural law and *Rechsstaatsdenken* are so different from the assumptions that used to be communist/socialist, but which is now more a general theory of social construction, that there is no bridge between them. We can therefore speak of different ideologies in a de-ideologized age – constructivism is not a specifically political ideology, but rather an extreme relativist position. Yet it has by now fundamental implications for politics. The 'advantage' that the natural law presumptions have now – in the fact that states have accepted international human rights as legally binding and the UN Declaration as the authoritative basis for these – can easily be eroded when (Western) states decide that these rights contradict their national public opinion.

In Norway we see an interesting polarization on this meta-political level, implicit in the political arguments used. There has been no natural law tradition in this country since the Reformation in 1536, and thus no continuation of realist philosophical thinking. The legal disciplines in Norway and Sweden are largely positivist – the famous Uppsala school founded by Professor Axel Hagerstrøm in the 1930s was premised on the dictum that 'ethics is about emotions and has nothing to do with law', as its founder is reputed to have put it. Law is the expression of majority will at any one time. In the Nordic countries the constitution is weak, almost a national icon, but of no political importance beyond symbolism. Some years ago, when a Lutheran pastor, Børre Knutsen, tried to invoke the Norwegian constitution's paragraph on the state being based on the Lutheran creed in a case in the Supreme Court on abortion, he lost. The constitution is not relevant, the court said. Few laws about controversial political principles are tried against the constitution. The *Rechtsstaat* is weak at the national level, but rulings from international courts, especially the ECHR in Strasbourg, are accepted as supra-national and now have direct conse-quences.

This little intellectual history serves to underline the importance of philosophical first principles – *Grundbegriffe* – for the terms of political discourse. Even if the debaters are entirely ignorant of their meta-political concepts, they argue from them implicitly. In the Norwegian case this is striking, as there are so very few who argue from a natural law understanding of human rights and law in general. The Catholic heritage is one of universalism in law – derived from the Roman law tradition and from realism in philosophy, whereas the nominalist Protestant tradition has been developed in the context of the state churches of Westphalian nation-states where all law and politics emanate from below. In the Norse political tradition, laws were decided on the *thing* (parliament) in Viking times where chieftains met. The Catholic Church introduced canon law, but when the Reformation ousted all remnants of Catholic legal life, the concept of a 'higher law' disap-peared altogether. The institutional presence of natural law was absent while the philosophical premises of such were non-existent.

This has led to a legal development in the North where law is entirely national, i.e. where there is no connection between the law of each state and a higher set of laws, unlike the states whose jurisprudence belongs to the Roman law tradition. The historical continuity of Roman law and the Catholic natural law tradition contrast sharply with the historical development of law and politics in the North.

The notion that states' legal systems are connected in terms of higher, general norms of law is entirely absent here. Only with the advent of international human rights in 1948 do we see such a connection, for these rights are based on the experience from the Nuremberg trials and the Second World War. There is immediate approval of the UNHR in the Nordic states and full acceptance of the ECHR of 1950. But this is typically a political acceptance rather than a legal one. The ECHR was only incorporated into Norwegian law in 1999.

There has been, and is still, a resistance to supranational law, based on both the nominalist premise of law and on the strong Westphalian state tradition. As long as international law, especially human rights, does not contravene Nordic politics, there is no problem between the national and the international level. Indeed, the Nordic states are major proponents of international human rights in the world. In the case of a seeming contradicton – as in the family case – the 'solution' is the constructivist argument, as we will se below.

Religious Freedom

The nation-state logic was based on forging one nation as the basis for a state. This required one identity, based on ethnicity, language, and/or religion. The ensuing identity was the very glue of the state, what held it together. The role of religion has been important as 'political glue', as has the other factors. The master nation-builder, Napoleon, saw that he must create Frenchmen and *citoyens* from an amalgam of peoples, languages, and cultures. The lack of a common religion after the Revolution was however so problematic that the revolutionaries, as we recall, made up their own God, to be worshipped as a substitute, and called him 'le grand Etre'.

In the Nordic states religion became one of the most important 'political glues', however: the state church merged God and state in hitherto unprecedented ways, and only in the late nineteenth century did we see the 'Law on Dissenters' which allowed non-Lutherans to stay in the country and to worship freely. Dissenters were those who held beliefs which were different from those of the established church. They could be tolerated, but only that, and those dissenters that were considered especially dangerous politically, were not allowed toleration: the Norwegian constitution contained a paragraph that read:

'Jews and Jesuits must not be tolerated and cannot enter the realm.' The Jews were allowed in in 1856, after much struggle by liberals; yet the Jesuits were not allowed in Norway until 1956 – the year before I was born.

Thus, we immediately see that 'dissenters' have had a hard time in many a European nation-state. In more pluri-religious regions religious freedom was much earlier in coming – the first instance of official religious freedom came in the dukedom of Transylvania (now Romania) in the balance between the Ottoman and Habsburg empires, in 1645 under Duke Gyorg Rakoczi. Calvinists, Lutherans, Catholics, Orthodox, Jews and Muslims were granted rights. In practical terms the empire solved issues like 'mixed marriages' by making sons follow their father's religion and daughters their mother's. This was still valid when my Hungarian husband was born to a Greek-Catholic mother and Lutheran father.

We also know that the long Turkish occupation of the old eastern parts of the empire, mostly Hungary, which lasted for 150 years, was conducted with tolerance of other faiths.

Religion and War

But religion is a powder keg when invoked for political rationales, and it is the most effective mobilizer of hatred when instrumentalized. This is not strange, it is logical: one's deep belief is the most important part of one's life and identity; one's commitment to the ultimate truth. This is much more than a political interest or a societal attachment; it reaches deepest of all in the human soul and mind. Therefore the rallying cry of Holy War can be so useful to a ruler or a 'conflict entrepreneur': it seems to provide a God-given seal on the righteous to fight the evils of this world, other people included.

All religion speaks about a holy war within the soul and a struggle for good over evil, against sin. In Catholic Christianity, which I know best as it is my own faith, the Christian is a *milites Christi*; a soldier of Christ, and life is a place where *mors et vita duello,* where death and life duels, as the medieval hymn *Dies Irae* graphically depicts. But the Christian must fight inside himself, and when fighting for the good in society, he must fight with peaceful means.

This is the great difference between the then and the now; between the time of the Crusades and physical wars in Europe, and the time we now live in where the Churches have left any claim to territorial power. When Jerusalem fell to the Christian Crusaders in 1099, it was a bloody massacre. Likewise, when the Muslims won in later battles, the bloodshed was gruesome. Religion was not only used to support territorial ambitions and war, but it was inseparable from politics: there were Muslim lands, or Christian lands. We should hasten to add that the view of human suffering and physical death was very different then from now. There was no modern separation of politics and religion. It was Christendom against the infidels.

This period of religious wars in European history was over with the end of the Thirty Years War in 1648. Thereafter the sovereign state was the rule; where the ruler decided on his subject's religion in the principle of *cujus regio, eius religio,* which ended the political claims to 'universal Christendom' in Europe. From now on the ruler decided on his own 'state' church, and also on whether dissenters should be allowed. It is however true that in many states religious minorities were already tolerated at this time.

The nation-state logic was the rule then, until now. What replaces it under our eyes today is the human rights logic where the OSCE, the EU and the COE play extremely important roles.

Human Rights: a Post-Second World War phenomenon

Human rights did not exist before 1948. By this I mean that they were not written down and solemnly proclaimed before that date. With the UN Declaration of Universal Human Rights we get the natural law document that states that the human being has 'inherent' and 'inalienable' human rights. In the legally binding European Convention of 1950 Europe gets a court to adjudicate on a supra-national level. These are revolutionary events, and we live in revolutionary times: the nation-state logic is being supplanted by the human rights logic: it is human rights which matter, not belonging to one 'nation'. Human rights is the universal ideology of today and tomorrow, and the political mechanism that makes them realizable, is democracy and rule of law – the latter the very specific mandate of the COE.

From this it follows that citizens of a state are no longer 'deficient' if they are outside the majority culture or religion; they are not 'dissenters' to be tolerated; they have equal human rights with everyone else; regardless of creed, race, and culture. True; there are majority creeds and majority cultures, and even 'state religions' (only in Norway, Monaco, and Liechtenstein as far as I can see today), but the basis for the state's legitimacy is no longer 'one nation'.

These are very sensitive and difficult matters, for they touch on identities that still exist as very strong. A recent article in *Foreign Policy*[1] by the famous Harvard political science professor Samuel Huntington illustrates exactly this.

Huntington, the father of the world-famous 'clash of civilizations'-thesis, writes that Hispanic immigrants in the US threaten to divide the US into 'two peoples, two cultures, and two languages' because they 'reject the Anglo-Protestant values that built the American dream'. In this article, remarkable for what it actually says along the lines of the nation-state logic, Huntington is appalled at the prospect of having a US with two official languages and a majority culture that is Hispanic rather than Anglo-Protestant. He goes very far in saying that the true

---

[1]   'Can you see, José?' by Samuel Huntington, *Foreign Policy*, March/April 2004.

American national identity is this one: white Protestant, and that groups that do not assimilate to this culture are a threat.

Huntington's fallacy – rare for a Harvard professor – is of course that he clings to the nation-state logic. This is also why his 'clash of civilizations'-thesis is wrong, for it puts the major emphasis on unchangeable cultural and religious traditions as if they were static and incapable of adjusting to modern democracy. In Europe we are in fact much more modern than in the US in this respect. We have states that are already multi-ethnic, multi-lingustic, multi-cultural and multi-religious. We are able to reject the argument that a state must rely on one national identity to exist. We have instead adopted more and more of the human rights logic as the basis of the state, not least thanks to the strong presence of human rights organizations like the ones mentioned. There is something pathetically old-fashioned about Huntington's fear of a Hispanic majority in the US: why should this be less 'American' than an Anglo-White Protestant majority?

The more we adopt the human rights logic, the less of a 'problem' this becomes. The norm in Europe is already societies with many nationalities, languages, and religions. This is also the fact in the US, and the US with its 'melting pot' should in fact be the very model for this.

The human rights logic implies that the state is based on respect for difference. The other is not those outside the state or the dissenters, but normal citizens with the same rights. They must contribute to the common good, to democratic co-existence, and the demands on citizenship will become larger than before because there is no 'national auto-pilot' to forge common values. The only values that form the common platform for the state are contained in human rights. This is a tall order; not easy, but the only way forward. It means that Islam must modernize to democracy and co-exist with it. This is I think fully possible, but it has not been tried yet – this democratic *aggiornamiento* is happening now and in the time ahead. Christianity has developed with democracy over centuries, in a European relationship where the spheres of religion and politics are separate and autonomous, yet inter-related in a specific way. The fact that democracy and politics is a sphere of society on its own is essential to both human rights, rule of law, and democracy itself.

There is no time here to elaborate on this theme, but I want to turn specifically to the human right of religious freedom and what it means.

Freedom of Religion and What it Implies

The role of religion under this logic looks very different from mere tolerance of dissenters. Article 18 of the Universal Declaration of Human Rights (UDHR) on religious freedom states that every human being has a right to public and private worship, to proselytize in public, to conversion, to have or not to have a faith. The human right of religious freedom is a very extensive and broadranging right. In addition, parents are entitled to, and have a duty to, teach their children in the faith of their choice and to choose schools for them in this regard.

The content of the human right of religious freedom is detailed in the OSCE texts. The OSCE has had to define how to apply religious freedom in non-democratic states, and makes it very clear that the state must allow great scope for religious activity. There can be no suppression of any religion, and every believer can have a public dimension of worship. Religion does not only belong to the private sphere, but can be proclaimed in public. It goes without saying that there are clashes with public opinion and often with state institutions. Many states desire to repress religions other than their own preferred one, and some religions do not accept that their members can convert or leave the faith, according to human rights.

I know of no religion which is not peaceful. By that I mean that sincere faith leads to peace, and to peaceful conflict resolution. The struggle is a spiritual one, not a physical one. In the Catholic Church, military power can only be employed in extreme situations of tyrannicide or self-defence. Those who preach holy war in a literal sense are usurping religion for their own political ends. It is the instrumentalisation, the perversion of religion.

Yet we see the effects of Islamic radicalism: the language of holy war, of infidels, of Muslim versus Christian, of good versus evil, has returned. It is really an old propaganda trick, and we see it throughout history, as in the time of the Crusades. I do not doubt that there are many such 'warriors' who are complete religious fanatics, and who really and truly believe that they are fighting for God's will. They are religious fanatics who have been indoctrinated. There have always been fanatics, and religion invites a certain fanaticism in many cases. It is easy to construct a Manichean world. Terrorists who commit suicide are in this category. They are irrational in the sense that they have no political plan or hope of a future. They are apocalyptic.

Yet many of those fanatics are not really such: they are what we call conflict entrepreneurs. In Bosnia and many other conflicts we have seen this clearly: paramilitaries have ignited hatred between ethnic groups by using religion as one cleavage point: in a state where Bosnian Muslims, Croat Catholics and Serb Orthodox had lived side by side in a sophisticated culture for centuries, Serb paramilitaries started the well-known technique of separating neighbours by ethnic criteria, sometimes forcing neighbours to kill each other so as to create fear and hatred. Extreme Serb and Croat nationalism was effectively propagandized. Even today, years after the war, fear has returned to multi-ethnic living. People are afraid to move back to their homeland.

I spent a lot of time working in the Balkans when I was state secretary. I have a special love for the beauty of Bosnia and its fascinating cultural history. It was, and is, a very sophisticated country on the 'fault line' between the Christian and the Muslim world. Many wars have been fought in this area, with religious pretexts. Two examples of interest on this topic must be mentioned.

Norway funded a lot of humanitarian help, *inter alia* a

so-called 'religious dialogue'. The clergy of the four faiths of Bosnia came together with us and talked. Fine and good. But when we wanted them to appear together in public, especially outside Sarajevo, they declined, at least some of them. This unwillingness was very regrettable, because we needed them to state that religion was NOT the cause the war. But it is still hard to get them together; often it is impossible outside the Norwegian embassy.

The lesson here is that religion can play a great role as peacemaker and moral authority – if the creeds stop distrusting each other. I grant that this is still early days after the devastating war, but the obstacles must be overcome.

The other issue I want to mention is history books in schools. For all our billions of kroner spent in Bosnia, we did not manage to have an effect on the most important factor, common history books. The schools are still Serb, Bosnian, and Croat – they do not have a common curriculum, least of all in the most important field – history. We know that nation-states in Europe were forged through common history lessons – the story of the nation, told from a national point of view. But how can Bosnians achieve something common as citizens if they are unable to agree on the history of the past?

Religious Dimension of Multi-cultural Education

The way to tolerance and peace goes through knowledge. Therefore the policy of the COE of inserting multi-religious education in the common curriculum is of extraordinary importance. It will have to be based on the human rights logic, as a right not only to be educated in your own faith, through normal catechesis. This is usually the province of churches and clergy in most states.

The education we talk about here is not catechesis. It is rather learning about what others believe, and why. The text books for this subject must be based on what religious representatives themselves decide is to be taught – there is no 'common synthesis' in any one book. Muslims must decide what Islam is and what is important to teach others, like Christians must decide what Christianity is. There is a teaching within each religion which is authoritative. Great stress must be put on dissemination and explanation, and on pupils' activities.

Let me say how important this is, how urgent it is: I read about a recent poll in the UK which says that Muslims are harassed and stigmatized because they are linked to the instrumental uses of religion by terrorists. The damage done by so-called radical Islamists is unimaginable. Muslims are in fact suffering collectively because some extreme fanatics misuse their religion. Against this the only effective way is knowledge, so that the European citizen can say: 'This is not Islam, for Islam teaches such and such about the use of force, and the taking of innocent life.' We could add examples from history where Christians also suffer from some group's use of religion for their own end.

The conflict entrepreneurs and the fanatics have often had an easy victory because people in general have been almost wholly ignorant of other religions but their own. Therefore prejudices about others have flourished: Catholics about Jews and Jews about Catholics, Christians about Muslims and Muslims against Christians, etc. The examples are legion. But consider how simple the explanation has been: never has there been much teaching about the 'others' in European states.

But now, in the post-national state; there are no 'others'. We are citizens of democracies based on human rights, not on religion or race. The COE can make a huge difference in consolidating this 'sea change' in Europe and in countering the all-too-easy perversion of religion for extremist agendas.

PART THREE:

CAN NATURAL LAW

BE RE-STATED?

CHAPTER SEVEN

CHRISTIANITY AND EUROPEAN DEMOCRACY

There is currently a very strong trend in Europe towards privatizing Christianity. This is the wrong, but easy way. It essentially implies that one can pursue Christianity as a private pursuit, like a hobby: some collect stamps; others are religious. Further, when everyone privatizes their religion, all can be happy in democracy, as there will be no clashes of religion. Law and politics will remain 'value neutral' and tolerant of all beliefs.

This model, so tantalizing, is not only unrealistic, but it is contrary to both religious freedom and to what democracy is really about. Article 18 of the UN's Universal Declaration of Human Rights (UDHR) states that religious activity implies public worship as well as activity to persuade others, and naturally this means that all religions will seek to influence the mores, i.e. the ethics of their society. In some religions there is in fact little difference between religion and politics – as in Islam – but in Christianity the very relationship between these two spheres is the essence of the European tradition, forged by primarily Catholic thinkers – a difference and yet an essential interconnection.

The relationship between specifically Christianity and specifically democracy is paradoxically the specifically European achievement that the Holy Father talks about.

There is a proper sphere for religion, which should never be interfered with by politics – as Article 18 also states – but there is also a proper relationship between the central Christian values and politics; for centuries the Church has taught that a political order which is not based on these values becomes an unjust order.

What is General Humanism and What is Specifically Christian?

What, then, are the key values that are specifically Christian, if any? These values are to a great extent reflected in the so-called natural law tradition and in the UDHR (1948), but I would argue that only the specifically Christian anthropology represents the importance of charity and self-giving so central to a society that purports not only to be just, but also good.

In other words, I argue that democracy in Europe (and elsewhere) should be founded on Christian anthropology, although many elements of this anthropology are also enshrined in the UDHR, which is in fact a natural law document. What is specifically and uniquely Christian, however, is the centrality of charity and self-giving in an anthropology centred on imitating Christ in all things. This goes beyond justice, to charity as the essential element.

There is therefore a duty incumbent on all Christians to influence society in the direction of these values. They do not belong in the private sphere, as there has to be a 'seamless web', or nothing. A Christian who ceases to be Christian in the public sphere is not very Christian and does not know his faith at all.

So far I have explained why Christianity has a comprehensive political and public side. If you accept this, I still have to convince you that the presence of Christian norms in public life is a 'matter of life or death'. I suggest that you accompany me on a little historical journey to the High North.

Around 1010 we find Olav Haraldsson, later St Olav; 'in viking', meaning at sea aimed at war, pillaging and vandalizing. He is on the Spanish coast, in Gibraltar. There, the saga tells us, he has a dream that he should return to Norway to introduce Christianity, 'the new faith', there.

He is one of many Norwegian pretenders to the throne who was sent to King Håkon Adalsteinsfostre (Ethelred) in England to be educated. In 1012 he is baptized by the Bishop of Rouen, and returns to Norway to Christianize the country and to bring it under his rule. He has fought Christian rulers along the Seine and in Normandy, but after his dream in Spain is apparently convinced that he has a divine mission.[1]

The key issue that faced Olav was that of a pagan society: how to change society into one that is based on Christian norms? He focused on the law as an expression of norms, and replaced the pagan law with *kristenretten*, literally the Christian law. He also placed Christianity squarely in the middle of society; not in any private sphere.

Some Norwegians at this time knew *Kvite-krist*, the 'White Christ' as he was called. There had been missionaries and an attempt to introduce the European faith before. But Norway and Iceland had remained outside the Roman Empire and the Vikings posed a military threat to Christian Europe. These countries were isolated, ruled by many competing chieftains; most of the local chieftains were pagan. They practised the 'blot', literally 'bleeding', the sacrifice of animals to the pagan God Odin, and had major 'blots' at midwinter, in the fall and in the summer.

[1] He ends his life as a martyr in 1030, being sancitfied some years later because of the miracles at his grave in Nidaros. In 1153 the Pope sends Cardinal Nicolas Breakespear, later Pope Hadrian IV, on the long journey to Nidaros, where he establishes an archbishopric that includes Iceland, parts of Scotland, the Orkneys, the Faroes and Greenland. About 100 years after Olav's death Nidaros had become one of Europe's major places of pilgrimage, and Olav had been canonized.

The sacrificial rites took place on the farms of the chieftains and when they met to make laws on the *thing*, the law-making assembly. Even today Nordic parliaments are named *things*, and our legislative districts in Norway have kept the Viking names to this very day.

The law was the centrepiece of society, the only order in a very dangerous and volatile anarchy.

The pagan sacrifice and lawmaking belonged together. The laws permitted what the Gods permitted: the *utbur*, meaning 'carrying out' into the wood children who were born ill or malformed; *frilleliv*, the life with several mistresses who had status similar to the wife and whose offspring were all pretenders to the inheritance of the father, and the taking of human life in revenge – an 'eye for an eye'.

Olav knew – and this is the key here – that introducing Christianity was not a matter in the private sphere; but on the contrary, it was a matter of *sidaskipti*, of changing the *Sitten* or the moral habits and customs of society. Therefore his main project was to introduce *kristenretten*, as law expressed the norms of society.

As could be expected, this was hardly a popular undertaking. Olav sailed from fiord to fiord, all along the Norwegian coast, fighting local chieftains everywhere. In most places they had kept the pagan sacrifices and customs. Olav gave them the ultimatum of changing sides or having their farms burnt. He besieged those who chose war, and gave privileges to those who chose the 'new faith' and let themselves be baptized. The emphasis was obviously not on inner conversion – that came later when priests educated abroad settled in Norway – but it was on changing the mores, the ethics – in short, the law – of society. This was extremely controversial: the common practice of infanticide was ingrained as was the men's privilege of sexual freedom. The Christian teaching on corporal fidelity seemed absurd, as did the indissolubility of marriage. Now the acceptance of a marriage became mutual – the bride herself had to accept it, not only her father. This 'women's liberation' that Christianity brought, ran contrary to the societal trends. The same goes for 'blood revenge', the primitive practice of killing your enemy. Christian teaching on forgiveness was seen as absurd in such a violent and militaristic society as that of the Norse Vikings.

Snorre, the great Icelandic historian, tells us in Olav's saga:

> He changed the laws on the advice of the most educated men, especially bishop Grimkjell and the priests; and he used all his power to abolish pagan laws and customs ... Several Icelanders were at court [these were the cultural elite in the North at that time] and he asked them in detail how Christianity was practised in Iceland. He thought that a lot was missing, because they told him that they still allowed setting out children to die, and to eat horsemeat, and to do other things that were against the new faith ... he also asked about the practice of Christianity in the Orkneys, the Faroes, and Shetland, and heard that it was practised in the same way. He spoke often about these things, about law and how to change it.[2]

The introduction of *kristenretten* in Norway and Iceland was really a matter of life or death when we consider how radical the 'right to life'-norm: no more infanticide, no more 'eye for an eye' or 'blood revenge', but rather an equality before the law in terms of human life. It could no longer be taken by the powerful at free will. The law, and the anthropology it embodied, was the key element of Christianizing these countries – the other of course being evangelization and the building of churches. The Norwegian author Sigrid Undset remarks that henceforth the Christian law was known as 'St Olav's Law', and was prefaced by the words:

> To the fount of our law, we shall kneel towards the east and pray to the holy Christ for peace and prosperity, and

---

[2] Olav den Helliges Saga, *Snorre Sturlasons Kongesagaer,* c.1200, published in modern Norwegian in 1979 by Gyldendal, Oslo, my translation.

keep our land well and be faithful to our king, with him to Christ, friend of all.[3]

The law that Olav fought physically to introduce on every *thing* throughout Norway and on Iceland, was the very basis for society and paved the way for Cardinal Breakespear's work about a hundred years later which consolidated the local laws and allegiance of the chieftains into one national *thing* and state council *Riksråd*.

There is a clear parallel to our time with regard to the 'matter of life or death': although the UDHR speaks of 'the right to life', the law allows abortion in most European states, and euthanasia is becoming legal in several states. It is also noteworthy that it seems to be Christians who are mostly concerned with this development. There are exceptions, naturally, but it is true that those groups who continue to oppose abortion and who warn most expressly in principled terms against the dangers of accepting euthanasia remain Christian. I believe that this is much due to our unique anthropology – different from all other religions and philosophies – in Christ's sacrifice for all on the Cross. The dignity of all human life has a very deep significance in Christianity.

I think this is where the importance of the public role of Christians becomes clear, and also decisive. First, it is clear by now that Christianity is meant to change not only individuals, but also society. This includes politics and law, although democracy has its proper rules and its proper pluralism.

Second, it is clear that the key Christian value of human dignity is one that causes scandal among men – as it did in Olav's time. Thus today there are signs of a new paganism, and the rejection of the central tenets of a Christian anthropology. In Olav's time, the strong prevailed, and the ill, handicapped and weak did not have equal dignity. Mercy and meekness had no place; nor charity or forgive-

---

[3]   *Norske Helgener*, (Norwegian Saints), S. Undset, Oslo, 1937, Aschehoug, p. 108.

ness. Similar tendencies are visible today: in the acceptance of euthanasia and abortion: in short in the gradation of human dignity. Christian anthropology introduced such revolutionary norms that the pagan Viking found it almost inconceivable with such an equality in terms of human worth. It is this unique view of man that is at the core of what we mean by 'Christian values' today.

After the Christianizing of Norway the country, like most other European states, remained Christian until a generation or two ago. Secularization is historically therefore a very new phenomenon. In this light it is indeed strange that anyone can oppose a reference to the formative role of Christianity in the EU's constitutional charter. This influence is a historical fact, whatever one may think of it.

'The Law Teaches'

There is an apparent dilemma today when we speak about Christian values and secularized Europe. On the one hand one cannot and should not impose Christian norms politically as was often the case in earlier times; on the other hand one should not privatize one's Christianity.

Clearly Olav's method is not good; it was not very charitable even by the standards of his own time. Today, however, neither the method nor the 'end product', the model of explicit 'Christian states', should be sought to be replicated.

On this point there is much simplistic thinking, also among Catholics. We must carefully respect the nuances of the question: first, there can be no Christian norms in society unless they are the result of persuasion and dissemination, and there can and should not be 'Christian states' in the old sense. Put differently, it is the deeper conviction that something which is true and right should mobilize the citizen to make it a general norm for all; and when something is right and true, it is necessarily right and true in *general*, as a universal, not solely as a Christian truth for Christians. There is no contradiction between reason and faith with regard to what the human being is and the definition and implications of human dignity. It is therefore not the idea to create 'Christian states', but to create states based on the truth about the human being.

There is much confusion and much manipulation about this: the key point of contestation is the concept of truth itself. If there is truth, then it exists independently of my subjective personal views of things. This is of course the position called ontological realism in philosophy. If one admits this, one then logically turns to the question of epistemology: how can we discover, how can we find, this truth? Then we enter into the realm of natural law: there are moral truths to be discovered because there is a human nature and a human dignity that is objective, and the way to use reason to discover what this truth is, is logical. It is the language of universals referred to above.

Here it simply does not make sense to talk about a Christian truth or a Norwegian truth or my truth – truth is either truth, or it is not. The concern of the Christian must therefore be to show, through reason and logic, that the very concept of law implies universal, i.e. moral, reasoning. But one can disagree, naturally, on how far moral reasoning leads. The specifically Christian anthropology is, as stated initially, *more* than natural law: conversion implies – and effects – a metamorphosis; a change into Christ-like life, and this surely has much deeper implications for society than law itself. Therefore this profounder change embraces, but goes far beyond, the legal and political sphere. It has, one could say, its own proper autonomy.

Pope Benedict XVI has repeatedly diagnosed the denial of truth as possibly the key problem in European politics and society today. This is absolutely correct. It is the assumption that truth is subjective and personal, as mere opinion, that prevents politics and law from functioning as they should. If politicians could agree that their ambit is about the common good, about universally right and wrong according to the standard of human dignity, then

European politics would look very different. The very denial of the existence of moral truths is the problem. The manipulation starts when majority rule is all that remains of democracy, and the role of the *Rechtsstaat* is undermined.

The political sphere, and especially democracy, has its own limits and own autonomy. There is a legitimate pluralism and there are several possible courses of political action on any one issue, where a Christian may opt for one or the other. However, there are some issues over which a Christian cannot compromise. Substantially these concern human dignity and what it implies; and also the dictum that politics and law are not unrelated to human anthropology, but 'derivatives' of it.

On this point we return to my initial remark on the uniqueness of Christianity and democracy; the European 'invention' and identity. It is precisely the freedom and autonomy of the political sphere that is at the centre of this, not in the manner of 'two regiments' living in separation from each other, but in the Thomistic sense of the relation between divine law and civil law where *who* man is, relates to *how* he should live in society. Ontology has implications for both epistemology and ethics, and therefore politics. This harks back to the master political scientist, Aristotle, who first formulated the key phrase of man being a *zoon politikon*, adopted much later by Thomas. The specific of Christian anthropology was also addded, building on the classical corpus.

'The law teaches', as Abraham Lincoln stated: politics and law are essentially moral; giving norms of behaviour for all. He opposed those who said that slavery could be enacted through majority voting, and his was a natural law argument. Not only a substantial argument, but also a logical one showing that the concept of law is related to moral reasoning.

The law is by definition universal – it lays down what is valid for all human beings – it is therefore concerned with what we call 'universals' in the language of philosophy. In contrast, if I make a contract to buy my colleague's boat, this legal act in no way suggests that everyone in Norway should have a boat or that it is right and good to have a boat (which it may be, but that belongs to the sphere of personal taste, not to moral rules). It is simply about a particular issue which therefore belongs in the private sphere.

The law, however, is logically bound to be about justice. When Olav changed the Norwegian law on infanticide, he laid down that it is not right to kill sick children. The punishment for doing so was incurred because infanticide is condemnable, and as such, a universal vice. The reason was the insight that Christian anthropology implied a human dignity that was equal to all humans. It was then perceived that killing the innocent was unjust. By contrast, a private legal contract concerns personal taste and choice: one would never say that it is condemnable that one does not buy a boat or that it is just or unjust.

Today the moral character of proper legal and political reasoning is strongly contested. In international law the dominant European school is the positivist one, and the view that political debate concerns personal viewpoints is also normal. Although one argues in the language of universals, e.g. that this or that is right or wrong, one does not admit that there are standards of right and wrong from which these terms take their substantial meaning. The ensuing paradox is that the language of politics in Europe today is highly moralistic, but the arguments are nonetheless nothing more than personal opinion: often one even uses phrases like 'I *feel* that this is right'. Politicians feel when they should reason according to logical rules.

In the political sphere, the Christian's first task today is to re-establish the nature of politics and the law. The first step is one of reintroducing logical reasoning: the language of universals, the moral language, is one about the truth of things: is this right, or wrong? Here natural law is the only viable road. Normative questions cannot be determined by majority voting, and posing the question of right and wrong in and of itself implies that there is a truth to be discovered.

The other main task for Christians is to show, by example, and explain, by words, what the Christian anthropology entails. This is an apostolic task, aimed at all fellow men, primarily at their personal level. This is both more important than, and primary to, the political task – and it is not the topic here.

Which Substantial Political Issues are Most Important?

Let me finally touch on substance. Which issues in European politics are the most important ones for a Christian?

I would say that there are four areas of special importance which can be summed up as the promotion of human rights: respect for human dignity as an absolute value; support for the family, also in economic terms; respect for the freedom of religion and churches; and national as well as international solidarity, also across generations.

In these areas Christians should be active: as voters, as citizens, as politicians, as moulders of public opinion. Let me attach some comments to each of these areas.

Human dignity

Today we see a particularly utilitarian tendency to see others in terms of their usefulness to us. We worship youth, beauty, effectiveness, and achievement in our societies. The old and the sick are sometimes barely tolerated. The unborn are invisible and therefore do not count, and the same often applies the old and sick. As family ties become less important in society, these people are thought to be the concern of the state rather than of our concern. It is very easy to rob them of their respect, which is their due as human beings. We must help society regain respect for the human person. This is the only way to combat abortion and euthanasia, as well as all other inroads made against human dignity in the field of genetic engineering and bioethics.

We must restore the sense of mystery and sacredness about the human being so that people will realize that a person is infinitely more than a heap of flesh and bones. There is a beauty, often hidden, about an old person or a sick person, but only an eye that sees the person beyond the body can discover this. All of us, at one time or another, realize that the other is our *Mitmensch* – our brother in a very real sense. Yet this ability to recognize all others as fellows must be trained and cultivated, lest it die to us.

I think the Christian in politics must act as a constant reminder of the existential fellowship of all people, regardless of the circumstances they are in. We must not remain indifferent to our fellows; yet it is very easy to show solidarity only with our kin.

We cannot hope for any new and more fruitful debate on abortion and euthanasia unless we succeed in this. After three decades of abortion on demand I find that most people are completely indifferent to the humanity of the fetus before three months' gestational age. It simply does not exist. Likewise, there is a large and growing indifference to old people – they are marginalized in terms of influence anyway. There are a tremendous number of lonely old people around.

Thus, we must be very aware of the tendency to talk about abortion and euthanasia as the only instances of disrespect for human dignity. We must never confine our concern only to these extreme instances. We are not credible in our defence of human dignity unless we also include a general commitment to solidarity with all, not least in the economic sense.

Solidarity

We do not respect human dignity if we allow for large discrepancies in economic and social welfare. Today market liberalism and its corollary, consumerism, are the key problems. There is the infamous gap which is widening between rich and poor states, but there is also more and more power vested in market actors to the detriment of political actors. We see this in global capitalism and we see it within each European state.

The labour force has lost bargaining power because capital has become global, and employers increasingly take in or lay off people with the fluctuations in the stockmarket. There seems to be no ethos whatsoever left on the part of the employer – short-term profit and not development that benefits employers and community alike, seems to be the only motive. This in turn makes it almost impossible for an employee to settle down and plan a family.

In my view capital has far too much power today. We know that the old socialist welfare state did not work, but we must not rescind on the concept of the welfare state. There is a clear need for the state to redistribute in order to attain economic justice within society. But in Europe today the picture is bleak in this respect: economic differences are widening and jobs are less secure than before. There has not been a good replacement for socialism in terms of welfare state thinking apart from Catholic social teaching. We need to put that teaching into practice.

Internationally, donor fatigue is rising. Fewer and fewer give less and less development aid. In addition, the values of materialism dominate us. It is indeed hard for a mother like me to fight the influence of the market on my children.

Christians must live solidarity in all aspects of life. Wealth creation must not be solely for oneself and one's family, but for the whole human community. Further, wealth is only a means, not an end, like all material possessions.

This is a hard lesson to practise. Most of us are very interested in material comfort and ownership. It gives an easy life and it gives status. We all desire this or that, and have to fight this dominant tendency all the time. For non-Christians it is even more difficult to realize that things are but a means to something else.

Today there is tremendous power in the market, and concomitantly less power in politics. We must fight to regain political power because the political is about the ordering of all of society, to which economics must be subordinate. With globalization this is much more difficult than in the era of the nation-state. But power comes to politics if and when we put our energy into it, disregarding our own private concerns about wealth. We can and must invest power in political institutions again – through your participation, and mine.

Christians must share in all senses, including the economic one. There is no mistake about the preference Christ had for the poor. Indeed, he was also one of them by his own choice.

Family

Today there are several challenges to the health of the family: unemployment and job insecurity for young people who are about to start a family; less political support for families and thus a weaker position for this institution; and a massive increase in divorces as well as individualism. It is no longer a foregone conclusion that one will marry and have a family, and the very concept of the family is itself being challenged.

We record that birth rates in Europe are very low, especially in Spain and Italy, but also in Eastern Europe. I like to boast that Norway has had one of the highest birth rates in Europe, and this is due to good social policies like a one-year paid maternity leave, paternity leave and job security for the mother when she returns to employment. The politicians in Europe must realize that today women are educated as well as or even better than men, and that consequently they both want to work – and usually have to work for economic reasons. In order to make it possible for the family to survive in Europe, we must have strong social and economic policies that protect it. Fathers must take their rightful share of housework and responsibility for the family.

This is also an age of tremendous individualism and little faith in the ability to stay married for a lifetime. Most people seem to want to try out marriage or at least cohabitation to see if it works, but not make any firm commitment. It is very easy to walk out, and this is fully accepted today by society's norms. Christians face a big challenge in trying to show the point of lifelong marriage. To most the idea sounds like a nightmare: to spend perhaps forty or fifty years with the same man or woman, losing one's precious freedom. How can anyone dare to make such vows? Why would anyone want to, anyway? Better to play it safe and retain the exit option.

A Norwegian author, Sigrid Undset, who has much inspired me, wrote as far back as in the 1920s that lenient marriage laws acted like a door which was always open, letting a constant draught into the home. The temptation to leave was always there, presenting itself as perfectly acceptable. Today this draught is like a gale force wind; almost no one speaks for lifelong marriage in public. True, it is easy to admit that stable marriage is good for both children and society, but will that argument convince the individualist of today? It is especially dangerous when public role models are 'trendsetters' in these issues.

Non-interference

This may seem a non-political issue, and perhaps it once was. Now, however, we have to restate the definitions of human rights instruments that define the freedom of religion and make sure that non-political spheres remain in society. Freedom of religion means that church teaching sometimes conflicts with public opinion and majority views in democracy. The right to deviate from public opinion must be ensured in practice, as it is in theory. Otherwise, majority views turn into majority tyranny.

Likewise, we must remind ourselves that there are non-political spheres of life and of society. These include civil society, family, and churches. The temptation to politicize these spheres is always there.

CHAPTER EIGHT

THE HUMAN RIGHTS POLITICS OF POPE JOHN PAUL II

I am not the evangeliser of democracy, I am the evangeliser of the Gospel. To the Gospel message, of course, belongs all the problems of human rights, and if democracy means human rights, then it also belongs to the message of the Church.

John Paul II, to journalists aboard the aeroplane to Pinochet's Chile in 1987

A Unique International Actor with a Unique Mission

The Holy See is a unique actor in international affairs in more ways than one. A legal entity on a par with states, accredited to most of the states in the world, with an equal number of embassies[1] accredited to the Holy See in Rome, it is a state-like entity but not a state in the normal sense. This actor is unique because its history is unique: the seat of the Pope and the Catholic Church, for centuries both the spiritual and the temporal centre of power in Europe. Now its power is purely spiritual, but its mandate is no

---

[1]   *Annuario Pontificio* ('Pontifical Yearbook'), Libreria Editrice Vaticana, 1999.

less impressive: the Church that Christ founded with Peter as the first Pope, continues its mission. For believers, the Church speaks the truth about the human being and his salvation; for unbelievers, the Pope and his foreign service play an important role in world politics as a moral corrective to pragmatic power politics. For those who intensely disagree with what the Pope says in the world arena, his contribution is nonetheless a clearly moral one in a world where such voices are rare.

The mandate of the Church and the Pope is by its very nature intensely controversial. First, it is claimed that there is a moral truth about human life and ethics, which in turn is to guide politics. Second, it is claimed that the full truth about the human being is to be found in the mystery of Christ, and only there. To unbelievers this is a folly and a cause for consternation in an age which questions the concept of truth and human nature as such. Never did politics seem to have less of a sure moral footing than today. And finally, the Pope and his government are not democratically elected. How can this entity called the Holy See be an international actor of considerable influence in the twenty-first century?

This chapter looks at the role of the Holy See in international affairs, in human rights and peace-making. Peace to the Catholic is not only absence of war – as it hardly can be for anyone – but it is the *just* peace: a peace which is permeating all of a society, based on a just distribution of goods, a just civil life where human rights are respected, and a process of justice for revealing the truth about atrocities that happened. The basis for the Pope's actions and statements in international affairs are always moral and ethical considerations of what is just and according to human dignity. These concepts are not subjective terms used for festive speeches, but form the very core of Catholic social teaching on which the foreign policy of the Holy See is based. The key importance of justice can be seen in such important traditions as the set of criteria for war, called the 'just war'-tradition, where St Thomas Aquinas of the twelfth century is still the major theorist.

The criteria of when it is justified to attack someone are relevant in the discussion about humanitarian intervention which has become the key debate in security policy these last few years. Likewise, the debate about when it is justified to take human life not only pertains to war, but also to civil society and the debate about abortion and euthanasia.

Thus, the contribution of the Church to ethical standards for political life continues to be of primary relevance, although Vatican diplomats are no strangers to the world of *Realpolitik*. They must know how to move politically in order to be useful in furthering their goals. Political work is about gaining power in order to achieve one's ends; but the ends vary greatly.

The Holy See was an international actor prior to the formation of states in the Westphalian system, being the see of the Catholic Church and the government of the Pope. The famous Roman curia simply means *court* – the court of the Pope. Today there are nine departments in this government, called dicasteries, and eleven pontifical councils,[2] composed of expert clergy and laymen from around the world. The secretariat of state is the core of the curia, and is divided into two sections, one of which is called the 'section for relations with states' – corresponding to a ministry for foreign affairs. It is led by the 'secretary for relations with states'. The diplomatic academy of the Holy See, referred to as *L'Accademia*, is considered the most eminent school in the world for diplomacy. One does not apply there, one is called to join. It is a well-known fact among career diplomats that the Holy See has perhaps the best practitioners in this ancient craft, not surprising in view of the long history of this institution. Much of modern diplomacy was developed several hundred years ago by these diplomats.

The Holy See – *Saint Siege, Santa sede*, is the government of the Catholic Church and recognized as a subject of

---

[2]   See the *Annuario Pontificio* 1999 for the details of the Roman curia.

international law. It is thus that the Holy See receives and sends ambassadors, not the Vatican. It represents close to one billion Catholics around the world, and is as such the only remaining actor which represents not a territory, but a religion. Functional representation in world politics naturally disappeared with the Westphalian state system, codified in the treaties of Westphalia of 1648 which laid down that sovereignty is tied to territory. But despite the strong emphasis on absolute rule by the sovereign king in his own territory, there were always exceptions to this: religious minorities were accorded some rights in many states in Europe (Krasner, 1999).

The Holy See represents the continuation of functional representation, crossing all territorial borders in its competence as sole agent for Catholics and for 'all people of good will'. It is understandable that such an actor is both misunderstood and rejected in a world where not only territorial states dominate completely, but where religious and spiritual values seem to lose influence. However, the Holy See is far from marginalized: on the contrary, rarely have we seen so much press attention to a Pope and so much interest in his statements. There is thus a delightful paradox in the fact that on the one hand the Holy See and all that it stands for seem antiquated and irrelevant; at the same time there is a tremendous interest in an actor at the centre of world affairs which speaks about human dignity and the human condition as being of essential importance to politics.

The Powers and Interests of the Holy See

Looking for 'national interests' of a traditional kind, one naturally finds none. The Holy See has no economic or military capacity or vested interests, although it has views on both themes. But there is no export interest to promote or military alliance to keep. As such, the Holy See is unique, as it does not have to observe the customary consequences of taking controversial positions. There are plenty of power pressures on the Holy See of course, and arm twisting is not an unknown factor. The interesting fact is that one does not have to yield to pressure. The consequences of not yielding are not fatal. They can be attacks in the press, criticism, and attempts at marginalization, but there is no leverage that any other actor has over the Holy See.

This in itself is a major power resource, as most if not all states have to take such repercussions into account. But the Holy See has used its freedom with audacity. For instance, before the UN Conference on Population and Development in Cairo in 1994, the US tried to pressure other states on the issue of abortion. Vice-President Al Gore sent a confidential memo to other states, putting strong pressure on them to follow the US policy line. The Holy See answered by publishing Gore's letter, which evidenced just this kind of arm twisting, in a press conference. One can imagine that such a move from a state with strong dependencies on the US would have led to repercussions, and that it therefore never would have happened. Another example is the Holy See's determination not to yield to pressure over its controversial stand on the sanctions against Iraq.

The powers of the Holy See and its leader are however based on much more than independence. The primary powers are those of appeal and persuasion, exercised in the public area. The growing importance of soft power in international affairs is discussed below.

Pope John Paul II, who was a former actor and a great media talent, chose the venue of public diplomacy for his office. An 'outsider' in the Vatican with a clear lay mentality and experience in managing the skills of political pressure from communist Poland, he opted for the public arena from the very beginning of his pontificate, combining this with the equally well developed skills of his diplomatic service. This combination proved a potent one in a world where 'shaming' as well as persuasion have become key power resources in the fight against transgressors of human rights and conflict entrepreneurs. John

Paul II chose an active role in world politics in the areas of peace-making and human rights like no other pope before him. He was the first to really use public diplomacy strategically; in terms of combining it with a skilled traditional diplomatic service; with selecting travel destinations where there are political as well as religious problems; and finally, in terms of using his press office and ordinary occasions for public statements very actively.

The Vatican has become a place where more than 300 journalists are accredited because the news broken here often comes first, as the gravitas of diplomats and commentators also shows. The news that can be had in and around the Vatican is interesting because the Vatican diplomatic service itself has access to information from every remote corner of the globe, through the system of the nuncio's[3] two-fold mission: to look after the local hierarchy and assist it, in addition to playing an ambassador's usual role. The nuncio's information flow is therefore from the most remote places in his country, through the hierarchical system of priests and bishops. The Vatican therefore has an unparalleled information source about local conditions, seen from the point of view of the inhabitants themselves and not from official presentations.

The Pope's public diplomacy is naturally not primarily a political performance, but a deeply pastoral one. Although he is formally a head of state, he makes his trips as a pastor – they are pastoral visits of a spiritual nature. However, they often have tremendous political implications, such as Poland in 1979, which inspired and 'awoke' the whole nation to seek freedom from Soviet rule; or the trip to Cuba in 1998 which brought world attention to Cuba for several days, and finally the trip to Israel in 2000; a major step towards a climate of peace and good will. The moving visit to the Holocaust shrine touched the hearts of the whole world. Peace and reconciliation work takes on a

---

[3]   The Pope's ambassadors are entitled 'papal nuncios', and in countries of Catholic tradtion they are the 'doyen' of the 'corps diplomatique'.

broader definition than just mediation: it encompasses the promotion of human rights, development, and democracy. This human security agenda is modern – it is similar to recent efforts at early conflict prevention and the need for integration of development assistance, good governance practices and political conditionality.

Thus, public diplomacy as we term it plays a key role in creating an impact for the Pope and the Holy See. To the believer, he makes an impact because they believe that he speaks as the Vicar of Christ, but for the majority he makes an impact for two other reasons: one, by appeal and persuasion – that he says things that are seen as just and right; and two, by 'shaming' and criticism, a political logic consistent with *Realpolitik*. Prior to and during a papal trip, or simply through a statement in Rome, maximum press attention is given to what the Pope says about a given political situation. The impact of being criticized when in such a prominent position has maximum effect an all but the hermits of this world. No political leader wants to bring this upon himself.

It is however the combination of public and classical, 'secret' diplomacy that was the most interesting aspect of the pontificate of Pope John Paul II. The Holy See's diplomats have always been skilled at their craft and connoisseurs of how to apply and use power. For instance, former secretary of state for relations with states Antonio Cardinal Casaroli was the very architect behind the rapprochement between East and West during the cold war; a policy much criticized by some Catholics as being a type of collaboration, but one which turned out to be the most prudent and wise in the given situation, given the need to keep up contact with Christians and their political rulers behind the Iron Curtain. Compromise is an essential part of the art of politics.

Classical diplomacy is done silently, gradually, as are most peace negotiations. The Holy See has been asked to mediate for two reasons: that it is a neutral and just actor; and that it is able to act discretely. Thus, the fact that the public arena is used does not imply that the classical diplomatic venues are less busy.

The interests of the Holy See are different from the conventional national interests of a state which primarily has to take care of its military and economic interests before it can turn to more common challenges and value questions. The powers of the Holy See are also different from those of a state: no military or economic power at all; only moral authority. Stalin's famous question: 'how many divisions does the Pope have?' had an unmistakably condescending ring to it, but Stalin turned out to be wrong then, and would have been even more wrong today. Pope John Paul II had considerable power in terms of *Realpolitik*; so much so that the Soviet politburo contemplated a plot against him in the first year of his pontificate, as Mikhail Gorbachev confirmed.[4] A classified document from the Central Committee of the Soviet Communist Party, dated 13 November 1979, was recently released. In it the Committee requested the KGB to study 'ultimate actions' along with publishing material that would discredit the Vatican and the Pope's 'activism', as it was termed. This was at the height of the cold war when Poland was slipping away, a process in which the Pope played a key role (Weigel, 1992 and 1999).

What Kind of Political Impact does the Pope have?

The statements of the Pope are naturally received differently by Catholics and non-Catholics. In a political perspective, however, it is the non-Catholics who are the most interesting. While the Holy See and the Pope act on their particular mandate and *raison d'être*, which is Christianity, their political statements and actions are intended for all people of good will, regardless of faith. Many will of course contest the conviction by Christians

---

4   'Soviets weighed plot against Pope, Gorbachev says', ZENITH news agency, Rome, 23 January 2001.

that there is no opposition between Christian ethics and the moral principles that should guide world politics, but this is an unimportant issue as long as these principles are accepted as valid. My point is simply that the Pope speaks to all, regardless of belief, and that his arguments must be judged on their own merits. The tradition called 'natural law' simply says that we can all discern what is right and wrong most of the time, and that you need not be Christian to be able to do this. The ethical principles that guide the political work of the Holy See and the Pope are just such natural law principles. One can justify most them in secular terms, although they are inspired by Christianity and based on the Christian view of man.

The public diplomacy of the Pope is not powerful because he is a Christian, but because his messages are accepted, or rejected, as valid and legitimate. The viewpoints on abortion, bioethics, and euthanasia, as well as on family issues, are often rejected by the modern Western public and press; the viewpoints on the use of military power, sanctions, solidarity, debt, workers' rights and human rights are often accepted as being deeply convincing and therefore right. Thus, even for non-believers, the impact of the Pope's public diplomacy is great, and its themes are those common to all politics: peace, human rights, freedom, democracy, justice.

In addition, there is the curious fact that here speaks the Pope, who claims to be the Vicar of Christ on earth, with a mandate no one else has; a mandate that is either true or false. This claim is so outrageous in the modern, relativistic world that it makes for tremendous interest and expectation of moral leadership and wisdom, of virtue, comfort, and love – despite the fact that few actually believe that the mandate is true. But the fact that one does not really know makes for a great interest in this person who is Pope, and for an expectation that he will act with the moral authority one would find in a man who really is the one he claims to be. The paradox is that while fewer and fewer in the West are able to believe that moral truths can exist, people still hunger for them, perhaps more than ever because everything has been declared subject to personal feelings and whims. I think this explains some of the magnetism of Pope John Paul II, but also of course the strong rejections of his message. However, the interest in value questions is a trend of international affairs – human rights, human security, humanitarian intervention – all these centre on the human being and on what is right and wrong, good or bad. These moral categories have suddenly become very relevant to post-cold war security policy, which is firmly tied to human rights, but which lacks both an adequate basis in the UN Security Council's mandate and in national, state-based security policy.

There is no doubt that the most important impact of the Holy See resides in the public diplomacy of the Pope himself. Where his message and appearance are accepted, the impact is tremendous. This 'spills over' into the political realm, where traditional mechanisms of applying political pressure are also used. For instance, prior to visiting St Louis in 1998 and having the routine meeting with the governor, the Pope asked for clemency for a man on death row, a Mr Meese, who was to be executed during his visit to the city. The answer was that the execution was deferred while the Pope was in the city, but would be done the week after. This was not satisfactory from an ethical point of view. Because public opinion in the US is so much in favour of capital punishment, the Pope decided that it would be more useful to use a discrete method. Upon leaving the cathedral after his Mass, he turned to the governor and simply said: 'Have mercy on Mr Meese'. Meese was granted clemency, for the first time in the governor's record.

But often public pressure is more efficient. One good example is the visit to Paraguay during general Stroessner's dictatorship. The night before, while the papal entourage was in Bolivia, Stroessner unilaterally cancelled the Pope's meeting with students and civil society – '*los constructores de la soceidad*'. This was conveyed by his chief of protocol to the Pope's spokesman, who went to the international news agencies, simply stating that 'for now we are surprised'. This was in reality a threat of cancelling the trip to Paraguay, and two hours later the meeting was back on the agenda. The representatives of civil society all met the Pope with hand-kerchiefs over their mouths – a telling signal of repression that was broadcast all over the world.

Visits are the best occasions for applying pressure, as one has sustained world media attention while the visit lasts. Afterwards Pope John Paul II followed up in the fight against the death penalty in the US by routinely asking for clemency for prisoners on death row, and making these requests public. This 'shaming' of US poli-cymakers cannot easily be undertaken by allied states or Western states alone, although the EU has started to publicly criticize the US practice. This issue is a sensitive one which divides Europe and the US, and one where the fear of repercussions keeps many European states more silent than they ought to be.

Thus, the statements made by Pope John Paul II, some-times sharp, mostly solemn, were accompanied by the often much more blunt statements by his spokesman. This led to popular mobilization for a cause and often to specific results. The time prior to a visit, when the terms of the visit are being negotiated, is also very good for getting political concessions, and the host does not want a cancel-lation or an embarrassment. Thus, the visit to Cuba hung in the balance until the last minute, when the Pope's spokesman went to see President Castro to demand the fulfilment of at least two conditions: that Christmas be celebrated that year with a day off from work, and that all papal events and Masses be broadcast in full on Cuban state TV. The negotiation between the two men lasted for seven hours through the night, until they decided on an outcome that satisfied the Pope.[5] The alternative would have been a cancelled trip.

---

[5]   Conversation with Dr Joaquin Navarro-Valls.

The Social Teaching: the Principles that Guide Political Action

The Holy See and the Pope work on a logic other than the interest-based one, and have other goals. These naturally derive from Christianity; from the mandate of the Church. Seen with secular eyes, one deals here with an actor; the Pope and his government, the Holy See, which act on a mandate they claim is given by Christ himself, and which contains the truth about the human being; what it means to be a human being, the rights and duties of the human being, and specifically, the relationship between the human being and the state. The human being's relation with God is the domain of theology, whereas the human being's relation to society and the state is the domain of what is technically known as the 'social teaching' of the Church.

This is an application of Christian ethics to political realities, developed over the last hundred years or so in a number of papal writings, known as encyclicals.[6] The social teaching forms the basis for the positions which the Holy See takes on various international problems, and is eminently practical, albeit rich in deep analysis. It is the Pontifical Council for Justice and Peace in the Vatican, where I am a member, which is charged with working on the social teaching, on developing it as well as applying it to new areas, but it is always the Pope himself who directs this work and makes decisions about it. The Council, like the rest of the curia, advises him. The Holy See, with all its dicasteries and councils, form the curia – the court – of the Pope, and does not and cannot act apart from him. In reality it is the Pope who makes all the important decisions, contrary to what many assume.

---

[6]   A good overview of the social teaching is found in the thematic anthology of papal encyclicals published by the Pontifical Council for Justice and Peace. *The Social Agenda: A Collection of Magisterial Texts*, edited by Fr Marciel Zieba, OP and Fr Robert Sirico, Libreria Editrice Vaticana, 2000.

The Social Teaching on International Affairs

The social teaching has in a way always existed, as the social and political implications of Christianity. For instance, the 'preferential option for the poor', a dictum of the political engagement of the Holy See, stems from Christ himself; born poor, choosing his disciples among the poor, and making statements reminding them that the poor would always be with them, having need for their care. The Sermon on the Mount cannot easily be ignored.

Likewise, peace is another great Christian theme which dictates that the Holy See works for peace in every situation. It does not imply pacifism, but it does imply a very critical attitude to the use of hard power and sanctions.

The dignity of the human being, the key theme of social teaching, also implies a number of things: that life cannot be taken by others except in self-defence and just wars; that capital punishment be abolished; that abortion and euthanasia are inadmissible, and that each person has a number of rights, such as the right to work, to a decent salary, to form a family, to educate one's children, to be politically active, and so on.

The social teaching refers to the body of papal encyclicals that emerged in response to major political issues in the nineteenth and twentieth centuries, starting with the debate over workers' rights in the 1880s. It is not possible or necessary to give a complete synopsis of the social teaching here; suffice it to say that the dignity of the human being, as a material but also primarily, a spiritual, being is at the core of the principles.

They all derive form this dignity, and demand that the person is free from interference and suppression by the state, that he is free to form a family, which is the basic cell of society and the place where human beings learn to love and are loved for their own sake. The state has obligations towards the citizen, and these include the very strong emphasis on the duty to provide work and social benefits in case there is no work. The state is to act to support its citizens when they need it, but not interfere in their lives

or in their families, churches, or other 'natural' associations – called the principle of subsidiarity: the type of
welfare envisioned by the state is not a socialist model.
However, the principle of subsidiarity is to be balanced by
the principle of solidarity, which means a radical solidarity with the poor and with the Third World. The papal
criticism of capitalism is sustained and unpopular in many
circles, especially among American liberals. In the writings of Pope John Paul II much attention was paid to the
dangers of 'consumerism', egoism, and materialism. In
certain respects the Pope's analysis of the alienation of the
human person under modern capitalism resembled that of
the young Karl Marx.

When considering the transition of societies from
communism, the importance of democracy, and conflict
resolution, we find an emphasis on freedom, democracy
with rule of law (*Rechtsstaat*), and an insistence on peaceful means of solving conflicts and on disarmament. There
is a strong involvement on the part of the Holy See on
issues such as small arms and light weapons, disarmament, conflict resolution, child soldiers, mine clearance
and peace operations, and the use of sanctions as a tool.
Likewise, there is a strong involvement in attempts to
create more just and better economic conditions in the
Third World, with a sustained campaign against Third
World debt.

The human rights approach has become a key feature
of the way the Holy See defines political themes, and the
Universal Declaration of Human Rights of 1948 sums up
the most important issues of the social teaching: the right
to life, to liberty, to security of person, to form a family
and to raise one's children, to religious freedom, to work,
to a just wage on which a family can be raised, to form
trade unions, to be active politically and to choose one's
form of government; to rule of law and a fair trial, and
so on. In fact, the Holy See has become a major promoter
of human rights – logically also because human nature is
the same everywhere, as is human dignity. Human rights
as such are therefore apolitical, pre-political and

unchangeable – universal, regardless of borders and powers.

The mandate of Pope John Paul II fitted the conditions of modern international public diplomacy perfectly: *human rights, democracy, values and justice.* These are the terms of public diplomacy today, and all actors in this arena have to command this language. But there are very few of them who are able to deliver a sustained and logical argument of an ideological nature on why human rights and democracy are essential to peace and justice. This ideology is the social teaching which is built on an explicit and reflected view of the human being and his relation to politics, both as actor and subject. The intellectual strength of the social teaching is important in the application to specific cases, to ensure consistency, which is often the Achilles heel of human rights politics.

The Ascent of Public Diplomacy and the Impact of the Holy See

This is the age of public diplomacy. Some issues can best be solved in secret channels behind the scenes, but the arena for influence, agenda-setting, and persuasion is the public one. Pope John Paul II was adept at using modern media, and chose such a public arena approach as his own. He travelled to more than ninety countries, commanding the entire world press attention for every trip, and was active in issuing statements at opportune moments through his weekly sermons or through his press office. These statements were timed to influence, and were often very controversial. The power of the public arena is the main power base of the Holy See, although as I argue below, it is the unique combination of public and classical diplomacy which made for the impact of this papacy.

When an issue is defined by the media, it is cast in terms of good versus bad, of personal rights versus state power; of moral duty to act. Then politicians cannot respond that 'we think immediate action brings no results' or that 'we shall consider the issue in all it aspects, but there is little our small country can do to really change anything'. The media set the agenda for political action once an issue is sufficiently politicized, and no politician under public pressure dares to opt out of action. One cannot be seen as defiant and reactive.

This logic, however, served Pope John Paul II. He did not have to defend any national interests or positions, had no dependencies where he needed to calculate, but was entirely free to act. Further, his terms of discourse were the normative ones, and no others. To him, politics was based on ethics and justice, and he applied the meaning of these terms to the case in question. Paradoxically perhaps, the very logic of media-based public diplomacy fits the ancient mandate of the Church.

The Pope's Public Diplomacy

The empirical treatment of this topic in a short chapter cannot pretend to be exhaustive, but I select some cases that illustrate the political impact of Pope John Paull II's use of the public arena.

Poland

The first important case is Poland and the transition to democracy. The traditional diplomacy of the Holy See was fully engaged[7] in the Helsinki process, as a full member of the Organization for Security and Cooperation in Europe (OSCE) and was *inter alia* largely responsible for the

---

[7]   The Holy See often chooses to be an observer, because of its special nature, to international organizations such as the UN, the EU, and the Council of Europe. Its contribution often consists of drafting of human rights texts where it has major expertise. In the OSCE the Holy See is a full member, and has been a central actor in the drafting process from the very beginning. The detailed texts on religious freedom can largely be accredited to its input.

important texts on religious freedom in these documents. In the OSCE one carefully developed human rights in politically binding texts that were agreed between the USSR and the West (Flynn and Farrell, 1999). The Helsinki Final Act of 1975 placed human rights on the same level as state sovereignty and non-intervention as principles of international affairs, and this gradually led to the empowerment of human rights groups in Central Europe (Thomas, 1999). The election of a Polish Pope was very unfortunate for the Soviet leadership, and his first visit to Poland sparked off a mass mobilization and social solidarity that was the major cause for the subsequent formation of Solidarity (Weigel, 1992; Thomas, 1999). The Polish episcopate strongly endorsed, according to the social teaching, the rights of workers to organize an independent trade union, and at a critical moment during the strike of the Gdansk shipyard's workers, led by Lech Walesa, the Pope used his Sunday sermon in St Peter's to defend the rights of the strikers (Weigel, 1999: 402).

The Pope continued to influence this process from Rome; for instance, amid the danger of a Soviet invasion of Poland in 1980 he sent a strongly worded letter to Leonid Brezhnev, where he again invoked the Helsinki Final Act's principles, but this time not the primacy of human rights, but the principle of non-intervention and state sovereignty for Poland.[8] This was the key principle that the Soviets had insisted on retaining, and which they invoked against human rights. Now the Pope turned their own key principle on them.

The just cause of individual and national freedom, of workers' right to organize, all flowed from the Christian view of man's dignity. They could not be classified as either Christian or political. They were both in its effects, but the basis was always Christianity and the primacy of the spiritual mission of the Church. On this point the

---

[8]   Letter to Leonid Brezhnev from Pope John Paul II, 16.12.1980, reproduced in Weigel, 1999, p. 406–7.

difference between the Pope and 'liberation theology' or any kind of politicized religion is clear; there are the political implications of the Gospel, but the Gospel is not primarily political. This interesting fact made the Pope able to act in any situation he deemed important. Communism was a political system that was profoundly anti-Christian in its materialistic anthropology and official atheism, but also in its undemocratic political system and lack of respect for human rights.

Chile

Another example of the impact of public diplomacy was the Pope's visit to Pinochet's Chile in 1987. Several Latin American states were in a slow transition to democracy in this period, but Chile was still under the military dictatorship of the general. In Santiago Pinochet attempted to use the Pope, including the arranged photo session on the presidential balcony, where it looked like the two leaders were posing together during a successful state visit. Such 'stunts' are of course normal if a Western leader visits a totalitarian state. But again the public platform and international attention was skilfully used by the Pope. Another event was arranged by the host: the riots during the main Mass, which disrupted the event and seemed to be the work of left-wing opposition, but which were in reality staged by the regime itself. The Mass exploded in police action and tear gas, intimidating all those present, but the Pope just continued the celebration.

The Pope used his method of mobilizing the people despite this; making the visit one which was visible to all, making them take to the streets for a joyous occasion and thus making it possible to gather for good and positive solidarity. In his speeches and sermons, he kept talking about the importance of democracy and human rights, and arranged a meeting with the opposition human rights groups in the nunciature. The left thought he was too timid in not calling for violent resistance, yet this was never his way. On the contrary, it was the same 'recipe' for political change everywhere: human rights include the right to have free and fair elections, and conflicts must be resolved peacefully. This flatly contradicts any pretence to keep power when it is not sanctioned by the people.

The Philippines

The first papal trip to the Philippines was in 1981, during the Marcos regime. Again people were mobilized for the values of the social teaching, and after the visit the Bishops' Conference launched incisive criticism of the lack of democracy and standards of human rights in the country. They issued a pastoral letter in 1983, 'A dialogue for Peace', which attacked the government directly on charges of corruption, violations of civil liberties, and mismanagement. At this time the opposition leader Benigno Aquino was assassinated; an event which sparked off massive demonstrations in the streets. This tense situation continued throughout 1984, when again the bishops wrote another letter attacking the government, and making specific mention of the Aquino murder. The rest of the story is familiar: more demonstrations, more government violence, a very active Church and Bishops' Conference; finally the acceptance of putting military leaders on trial for the Aquino murder, and a subsequent election for president where Aquino's widow, Corazon, stepped forward as a candidate. During the fraudulent elections, Cardinal Sin maintained a leading role in instructing the people and in exposing the Marcos government. Marcos declared his own victory after a totally fraudulent election, while the cardinal and the bishops issued a statement denouncing the election as invalid and calling for a non-violent revolution. The Vatican nuncio and the secretariat of state in Rome were not all of one mind about this turn of events and the active role in national politics of the president, but all could see that there are moments in history where the just option is one where the pastor has to lead the people in practical, political action.

The Philippino revolution was successful and non-violent, and its leader had been a Catholic cardinal, urged on from Rome by the Pope if not by all of his diplomats.

Human Rights at the UN

Two UN conferences in the 1990s stand out as being of particular importance to the public diplomacy of the Holy See although it participated actively at all of them.

The first is Cairo in 1994, the World Conference on Population and Development. Here the issue of abortion came to the fore as a possible means of family planning; a horror to the Pope because it put in jeopardy the whole issue of the right to life, especially the right to life of the very poorest in the developing world. Here the confrontation was between the most powerful state in the world, the US, allied with most of the Western world, and the Holy See and some Latin American, Middle East and Third World states. The Pope saw the Clinton agenda for promoting an international abortion right at an early stage, and decided to launch a counter-campaign. He addressed the *corps diplomatique* in Rome, and used the daily *angelus* meditation to speak about the sanctity of human life, while his spokesman used much more blunt language in exposing the US definition of 'reproductive rights', which included abortion. While the vice-president Al Gore flatly denied that this was the case, the former gave a press conference in Rome producing evidence that he was in fact lying. This was an unprecedented move, and one which showed the Pope's total willingness to face full confrontation on this issue which was of vital importance to Christianity. The ensuing conference in Cairo was no less confrontational, with the Holy See delegation holding up final agreement for a full week in order to get rid of the reference to abortion as a means of family planning. They succeeded at this, but were seen by many as difficult and punching above their weight and by others as being the principled defenders of life.

At the Beijing World Conference on Women in the

following year, there were similar issues and confrontations: abortion, the right to life, the equality of women in poor and rich countries, and so forth. In this conference, where I was one of the Holy See negotiators, we actively used public diplomacy. Seeing that many European delegations acted in ways that could not represent their national public opinions, we issued a press statement on the first Sunday of the conference, which is the time when the news agencies have least news, asking whether the Spanish, Italian, French delegates, etc. had any mandate from their national constituencies for the radical positions they voiced in the negotiations, citing some of them as examples although what went on in the negotiations was formally confidential. This press statement received top headlines in the European press, leading to formal questions being posed in many national parliaments. We had the added advantage that most European states made up the EU delegation, speaking with one voice and hence not reflecting the national positions of states per se. Using public diplomacy at UN conferences in this way was unprecedented, as most delegations did not even have a press spokesman. Ours, the hard-hitting Navarro-Valls, spent time in a lot of press rooms, giving analysis and viewpoints to the world press assembled there. They, on their part, were always hungry for something to write home about.

The multilateral diplomacy of the UN conferences is about public opinion and about text formulation. The latter is important for the human rights definitions of the UN, and for the Holy See this was of key importance because much of the battle over ideas in international politics today is about life, family, dignity – the 'lifestyle issues' that concern us all. The powers of the Holy See in this context were certainly public diplomacy and skill at drafting human rights texts, which operate with a logic of their own, like most such texts. Sheer national power must command this skill in order to succeed in such negotiations.

Cuba

Another candidate country for transition to democracy and rule of law is Cuba. For a long time, the Pope had wanted to visit, and there had been various tensions between the Holy See and Cuba for many years: the local bishops criticized the regime in their pastoral letters; the regime harassed the Church in typical communist ways: for instance denying the right to own a printing press, or the arrangement of a religious feast day. There were exchanges of visits, by Cardinal Etchegaray and the secretary of state Tauran, who was kept waiting half the night for a nocturnal meeting with Castro, only to have him deliver a three-hour harangue. This kind of interchange continued for several years, and the situation for the Church and for general human rights continued to deteriorate. There was no media access so Christianity was invisible; there were persecutions and several hundred political prisoners, and little progress to be seen. However, when Castro went to the World Food Summit in Rome in 1996, he was received by the Pope and he issued an invitation for the Pope to visit Cuba. There were plenty of hard negotiations ahead, about the terms of the visit, which continued up to the last minute. The Holy See demanded full media coverage of the visit and the Masses on Cuban TV, visas for nuns and priests, the granting of Christmas Day as a holiday and the acceptance of Christmas celebrations. While in Cuba the Pope denounced the US embargo of Cuba; an important point for Castro but also one that was a genuinely held conviction on the part of the Holy See. Having put pressure on the US, it is noteworthy that the food and medicine parts of the embargo were lifted after the Pope's visit. Moreover, the most important impact of the visit must have been the 2000 journalists, also many from the US, who descended on Cuba. 250 political prisoners, a list of which was submitted as a complete surprise to the Cuban MFA during the visit, were also released during the following months.

After the exhilaration of the visit, there were no major regime changes, but as the only independent source of power in Cuba the Church had been strengthened by the publicity received. Cuba was on the agenda internationally in a new way. Two countries, Canada and Norway, started national human rights dialogues with Cuba. The Norwegian dialogue, which I initiated, built on the contacts with church representatives through the Holy See as well as the Norwegian socialist legacy of contacts with the Communist Party. The Cubans, extremely sensitive to criticism, broke off the dialogue with Canada after Jean Chretien's visit during which he made some critical remarks about the slow pace of reforms on human rights and the imprisonment of some dissidents, and they also broke off the Norwegian dialogue in 2000 after Norway abstained on a resolution critical of Cuba in the UN's Human Rights Commission. This dialogue was however soon back on track, but one must ask whether the Cuban reactions served their interests. It would be more useful for them to retain the dialogues when being criticized by the international community.

The impact of the papal visit to Cuba was not revolutionary, but evolutionary. Things happen at a slow pace as long as the embargo effectively blocks off the island from normal contacts and trade, and equally important, keeps Castro in power. But contact through a multi-faceted dialogue with various groups in Cuba, including projects and cooperation with the churches, is an investment for the longer term, for post-Castro Cuba which by necessity will come in the not-too-distant future.

Peace Mediation and Facilitation

Beagle Island Channel

The issue of peace is tied to human rights; there can be no true peace without truth about right and wrong, and respect for human rights. This connection has inspired the work of the Holy See in international affairs. Over the centuries there have been many direct, secret or open, peace negotiations. The last one I know about before the pontificate of Pope John Paul II was the dispute between France and Germany over the Caroline Islands in 1885. However, immediately after his election, John Paul II took a chance and dispatched an envoy to attempt a mediation between Chile and Argentina over the Beagle Island Channel. This he did on his own initiative, in December 1978, sending Cardinal Antonio Samore. At that point the conflict was almost turning into a war, and the Pope later said that he felt compelled to try everything to prevent two Catholic states from fighting each other. After the cardinal's shuttle, the two states asked for an official mediation by the Vatican. This resulted in the completion of the Treaty of Montevideo in 1985.

The Balkans

There was then a continued effort to assist in resolving the crisis in Bosnia 1992–95. The Pope sent Mgr Vicenzo Paglia, member of the layman's peace mediation group *Communita di Sant' Egidio*[9] to all the Balkan capitals in

---

[9]   This community has peace mediation as its main task. Not related directly to the Holy See apart from being an acknowledged lay community, of which there are many in the Church, the Sant' Egidio has developed probably the world's best expertise on the Balkans and in certain African conflicts (Burundi, Congo). The community's work in both places has been and is financed *inter alia* by the Norwegian goverment, and Mgr Paglia had extensive contacts with both the Milosevic couple as well as with Albanian leaders. He managed to negotiate a school and university agreement in Kosovo in 1998–99, but, due to Serb non-compliance, this was not implemented. Afterwards the conflict escalated, and the military campaign set in. Prior to this, however, the US secretary of state Madeline Albright came to the community's HQ in Trastevere in Rome to consult with Mgr Paglia. She did not, however, heed his advice, which was against the military campaign. The Pope had close relations with Sant' Egidio, and they also went to Belgrade during the bombing in an attempt to start mediation.

order to prepare a visit. This mission led to an invitation to the Pope from all capitals except Sarajevo, but in Belgrade the orthodox bishops were in two minds, and that leg of the trip was cancelled. The Pope was however adamant that he should go, especially to Sarajevo, and kept his advisors aware of his intention. Despite advice to the contrary, he insisted on being with the people of the city under siege, and tried all possible means to get there. I know that he was the one who kept demanding to go, despite the advice from many of the people around him. Finally a trip was set up, but at the last minute Radovan Karadzic, then Serb commander in Pale above Sarajevo, refused to grant the necessary security guarantees. He said, in reality, that his soldiers would not shoot at the Pope, but that they would not guarantee the safety of the people. In an outdoor Mass in Sarajevo stadium this could have meant an open-air massacre from Mount Igman.

The Pope was extremely upset at this move, and deeply sad on behalf of the besieged population that he so much wanted to be with in solidarity and in order to draw press attention to their plight.

Sri Lanka

Other peace engagements include an initiative on Sri Lanka in 1998, when I was Norwegian state secretary and asked by the Holy See to engage Norway as a peace mediator in this long-standing conflict. This idea was not foreign to Norway at the time, as we had extensive aid and long-term connections with the government in Colombo, whereas the Holy See had direct contacts with the guerrilla leader of the Liberation Tigers of Tamil Eelam in the jungle in the north. They therefore could assist in this side of the conflict. Soon thereafter the government in Colombo asked Norway to facilitate, a role it still has at present.

East Timor

Other conflicts where the Church has played prominent roles include the difficult balancing act in East Timor where Bishop Belo of Dili tried for many years to avoid political involvement, and to mediate qua pastor only in the tense situation. The Holy See kept a prudent and careful balance between putting pressure on Djakarta and encouraging the East Timorese to act. The final resolution of this conflict owes a lot to the bishops in East Timor and to their very quiet way of working on this long-standing conflict. Norway also assisted in this work, in a quiet way, in collaboration with Bishop Belo.

Guatemala

Mention should also be made of the post-conflict human rights commission work and the important effort at revealing truth in Guatemala. The work of the late Archbishop Gerardi stands out in this regard. Norway had worked closely with the Church on both the peace settlement and later on the follow-up. The idea of a human rights commission was important, and Norway undertook to finance its work. Its president became the respected and loved Archbishop. When the commission's report was published by him in 1998 he was found slain some few days later. The murderer was never caught. The Archbishop obviously knew too much, and he also knew what risks he took. The reconciliation in Guatemala continues, but at a great loss.

Apart from his nuncios and the occasional use of the Sant' Egidio community, the Pope used the Basque Cardinal Etchegaray as a kind of universal 'troubleshooter' in hot spots around the world. The Cardinal, who held the position of the president of the Pontifical Council for Justice and Peace, was sent to all such places as the special envoy of the Pope. Thus, the Pope used several venues for conflict resolution, and often the non-official yet official envoy, with an unspecified mandate, can be crucial in tense situations where good contacts with all sides matter most.

Sanctions and War

The Holy See's views on the use of hard power, sanctions and military might were highly controversial and interesting at a time when both these most serious instruments of international politics were being debated at the UN and elsewhere. The US Secretary of State Colin Powell started his term in office by declaring that US unilateral sanctions would be reviewed, and the ten-year-long UN sanctions against Iraq were seriously discussed in the world community.

Likewise, the use of military power is now under major debate. The practice of the UN Security Council (UNSC) throughout the 1990s was one of uniting human rights concerns, often termed 'humanitarian concerns', closely to the Charter's Chapter VII and its mandate which requires the existence of a 'threat to international peace and security'. Such a diagnostic has been used in the cases of South Africa (res. 418/77); Iraq (res. 688/91); Bosnia (res. 770/92); Somalia (res. 733/92); Rwanda (res. 929/94); Kosovo (res. 1199/98 – which did not explicitly sanction the use of force, however); and in the case of Haiti in 1994 the UNSC even declared that the *coup d'etat* was such a security threat and mandated the use of military means to reinstitute democracy (res. 940/94).

The problem with the practice of the UNSC is that on the one hand it is clear that human concerns and human rights form the core of the modern war, an armed conflict where civilians suffer as both victims and protagonists; on the other hand it is equally clear that the UNSC may be used to gain legitimacy for invasions by the mighty states, in other words the US. The Haiti mandate was close to this kind of situation, and the Kosovo air campaign was not fully mandated by the UNSC, despite coming close to it.

Given the importance of massive human rights violations in modern armed conflicts, one should expect the Holy See to favour the use of force for such good reasons. The stance on sanctions has been firmly negative, as this tool hits civilians. The stance on the use of force has been careful, often negative, but also clear on the need to disarm the aggressor, a key principle of the 'just war' tradition.

The position on the invasion of Iraq was that while the Iraqi invasion of Kuwait involved a major transgression of international law, one should try everything to find a peaceful solution to the crisis. Resorting to military power was to be the last resort. The Pope made dozens of appeals along these lines during the autumn of 1990, and when it became clear that there would be a resolution through a war, he renewed this request with more urgency. There was criticism of this line; one asked whether the Pope was a pacifist.

But this was not the case. The reason for the constant insistence on peaceful conflict resolution seems to have been the Pope's conviction that his role was that of reminding policy-makers of the moral principles that ought to guide them, and not to provide a defence of the use of force according to the just-war tradition. Judged by the latter's criteria, using force against Iraq certainly would be justified: it invaded a small neighbour, it was ruled by a dictator who used nerve gas on his own population, and this ruler was a threat to the entire region. But this analysis is the task of the politician in charge of making the decision. Only he or she knows all the facts of the situation.

On the sanctions issue, the Holy See's negative stance seems to be borne out by the facts. Always and on principle opposed to the use of sanctions because it affects innocent civilians, the Pope spoke against the Iraq sanctions as well as others, such as Cuba. In the case of Iraq, he repeatedly denounced the sanctions for their effects on civilians, something which now seems a more widespread view in the international community, but a stance which was vehemently opposed by the US and the UK.

In Kosovo the UNSC did not have a sufficient mandate for military action, but NATO acted on a combination of prior UNSC resolutions and the gravity of the humanitarian situation. Again the Holy See was heard as being the promoter of more negotiations, but the Pope also said that an aggressor must be disarmed. Mgr Paglia, the principle Balkan expert of the *Communita di Sant' Egidio* and the Pope's adviser, was angered by the bombing. It would not solve anything, just compound the difficulties, he said. He also thought the Rambouillet negotiations had put unreasonable demands on the Serbs.

At the time I was Norwegian state secretary, and in favour of the military campaign, which I still am today. Seeing the mounting harassment of the Kosovars of which, as the chairman of the OSCE in 1999 and therefore in charge of the Kosovo Verification Mission (KVM) I had first-hand information, I saw the logic of war as inevitable. We had tried every diplomatic move, and Milosevic still made major troop movements into Kosovo, and the incidents of ethnic harassment, this time violent, increased. But the Kosovars also armed and built up their own guerrilla army, the KLA. The street price of Kalashnikovs had reached 200 dollars on my last visit to Tirana just before the bombing started, and then I knew that they were in great demand across the border. Usually they could be had for fifty dollars. 'War has its own logic', foreign minister Tauran had told me. That was certainly true.

Conclusion: The Just Peace; rarely The Just War

I do not know the specific reason why the Pope and the Holy See confined their role to promoting the just peace through democracy, rule of law, development aid and human rights as the *sine qua non* of the good society. The Pope could also have provided the world with an application of the traditional criteria of the just war when the international community discussed exactly when the use of force could be legitimate. I can, however, see two explanations for this.

First, the just war criteria are not specific enough to be applied with precision to a given case of escalating conflict. It is easy to analyse such a case with the hindsight of knowledge and experience, but almost impossible in the heat of a tense situation unfolding from minute to minute. If the Pope, as the foremost moral authority on the world scene, were to provide such an analysis, the consequences of making an error of empirical judgement would be great, as his 'yes' or 'no' would be used by all sides for their own purposes.

Second, the more profound reason is, I think, this: the Pope is not a foreign policy maker. He is a pastor, not a politician, despite all the political consequences of the Gospel. The task proper to a pastor is to preach the necessity of peace, not to encourage or sanction war. Imitating Christ, the Pope does not enter into the role of the secular ruler, but keeps to the message that can be derived from the Gospel message. Those of us who are or have been foreign policy makers, however, have another role and responsibility, which may also include the use of force in extreme cases. It is therefore our task, as normal, upright politicians and citizens to do the analysis of the just war criteria when we are faced with a choice to be made about the possible use of the ultimate means of international politics. I supported both the Iraq war and the attack on Kosovo, judging from all the information that I had about them, but also analysing my decision in terms of the ethics of the matter. This is the task proper to the politician who has to act on the situation and carry the consequences for either course of action.

To sum up, Pope John Paul II's efforts at promoting human rights and the just peace grew out of his pastoral responsibility, and he chose a more active role in this endeavour than any other Pope before him. The Holy See's classical diplomacy certainly does a lot to work for this kind of peace, while the Pope excelled at public diplomacy. In combination this makes for much soft power, despite the almost total lack of other means of power. The uniqueness of the Pope and the Holy See notwithstanding, there are some general implications here for international relations theory: that small actors, public diplomacy and soft power can be of great significance, and that legitimacy and persuasion are key variables for wielding influence in modern politics.

CHAPTER NINE:

POPE BENEDICT XVI: THE 'TYRANNY OF RELATIVISM' AND ITS RATIONAL REMEDY

In this book we have visited and re-visited the problem of truth and democracy under various guises. We have argued that there is a vital difference between pluralism and relativism – the former a hallmark of democracy, the latter a threat to democracy. We have also argued that Western democracy today faces a relativist challenge in the form of nihilism which threatens to undermine both democracy and its core values, expressed in human rights.

Two contemporary intellectuals in Europe stand out as contributors to the debate on this issue. They are both professors – Jurgen Habermas of sociology; Joseph Ratzinger of theology. The debate between them is vested in different views of metaphysics: whereas Habermas argues that we now live in a definite state of post-metaphysics; i.e. that metaphysics is no longer a possibility, Ratzinger argues the opposite viewpoint. He concludes that rationality is not possible without a metaphysical grounding.

Metaphysics is nothing more mysterious than knowledge of human nature and the concomitant ability to use reason to discern fact from fiction, truth from falsehood, and right from wrong. In the classical tradition, human nature and its rational ability was the point of departure, and the sciences that dealt with these aspects of life were termed 'above physics', i.e. meta-physical. Physics, mathematics, and logic were sciences based on meta-physics – one could not, for example, have logic without a rational human nature.

Before we turn to the argument for metaphysics and natural law, let us take a look at the contemporary debate.

Habermas asks how consensus can be established in the absence of truth, as truth is not possible, especially in the ethical sphere. His answer is that rational dialogue is the way, an ideal and a possibility between rationality-seeking individuals who try to free themselves from all power structures and interests. The need to shed interest from knowledge runs like a red thread through the extensive scholarship of Habermas (*Erkenntnis und Interesse*, 1968) as does the analysis of material and immaterial power structures in society (*Strukturwandel der Öffentlichkeit*, 1962). Habermas' well-known call for a *herrschaftsfreier dialog* as the precondition for rationality is embraced by all who seek a free and open public debate.

But this hypothesis rests on the condition that it is indeed possible to act as a disinterested citizen. This is contested by many, but it is not, in my opinion, the main problem with this otherwise very profound proposal.

The logic of the interest-free dialogue as the replacement of the search for truth is clear enough in a society which has abolished the truth claim, but it can never lead to a substitute for truth. From time to time, the Norwegian research council, undoubtedly using the same logic, arranges so-called 'consensus conferences' on controversial topics, such as biotechnology or feminism. The logic is Habermasian: through open and 'interest-free' dialogue one will eventually arrive at a consensus in the field. This will be the only truth available, based on an inductive process whereby compromise is the logic. But is induction and compromise anything more than the political 'art of the possible'?

If we are dissatisfied with the Habermasian solution, is there an alternative? Can one reason rationally about normative matters as one can about natural science? Is the problem today really one of a reductionist notion of rationality?

This is the thesis of Professor Ratzinger which he expounds on in various books, talks, and articles.[1] His major point is that modern rationality is limited and impoverished, and that we need to rediscover classical rationality in order to understand what the human being really is. Only a correct understanding of the human being can form the basis for democracy and human rights.

Let us examine his analysis.

The major problem with modern European society is, according to Ratzinger, the limitation in the understanding of rationality. While there has been tremendous progress in natural science since the Renaissance and most importantly, the Enlightenment, there has been no progress in what one can call 'the moral sciences': 'Morality has not progressed, rather regressed because it is relegated to the subjective sphere.'[2] Rationality, says Ratzinger, has become defined as 'functional rationality', which is the *Zweckrationalitat* of a Max Weber: does something work to the end we need it for?

This is a wholly legitimate form of rationality, but it is nonetheless limited. At the same time there are of course values which are more and more talked about in society – it seems that there has never been more talk about values and ethics – but these are defined in a wholly subjective manner and easily become instruments of political correctness. There is more and more moralism in both politics and theology, says Ratzinger, but this is uninteresting and

---

[1]   These are not statements made from the prefect of the Congregation of the Doctrine of the faith, Cardinal Ratzinger, or from Pope Benedict XVI, but are arguments from the professor and the intellectual.

[2]   'Europa in der Krise der Kulturen', Acceptance speech for the Premio san Benedetto 2005; Monastero di Santa Scolastica, Subiaco, 1 April, published by the abbey as a book, *L'Europa nella crisi delle culture*. Editione Cantagalli, Siena, p. 48.

anti-intellectual as long as it remains a matter of feeling and subjectivism. The political moralism of the 70s was 'a type of moralism only, as it was irrational ...'[3]

Rationality is the key word for Ratzinger. He returns to the limits of functional rationality: 'only that which can be measured is rational'.[4] But the experiment as the proper method of natural science is not the proper method of philosophy of theology, and no one would expect it to be so. However, proponents of the latter disciplines have failed to show their rational roots, roots that necessarily must be grounded in insight about the human being. But while Immanuel Kant could still propose a category of the good – *an Sich* – and the categorical imperative as an axiom, this is no longer possible, says Ratzinger. Modern Europe, which has been both the culture of philosophy and theology as we know them, has also produced their anti-thesis, which is the dominant culture of instrumental rationality of today where any knowledge about the human being is mere whim or subjective feeling.

What are the limits of the rationality we possess today, viz. instrumental rationality? In an incisive logical argument he puts forward the hypothesis that current European instrumental rationality cannot serve as a universal paradigm. It is only in Europe that moral norms and religion have been banned from the public life of nations in a rather crass version of secularism. But this secularism puts itself forward as the only valid one against which to measure other cultures and civilizations, thereby making a mockery of its respect for pluralism and relativism. The only thing that is not allowed to be criticized in the name of relativism is this very European culture itself. The European paradigm becomes the only politically correct one, thereby committing the logical fallacy of assuming that one set of values is more valid than another

[3]   Ibid., p. 49
[4]   Ibid.

without admitting that it must then be based on an objective set of values.

A good example of this is the debate around the publication of drawings of the Prophet Muhammad in February 2006. These caricatures were first published in the Danish newspaper *Jyllands-Posten* and later in a right-wing Christian publication in Norway. The reactions were fierce, from boycotts to the burning of embassies in the Middle East. However, in the Nordic countries the debate about freedom of expression with regard to this case is highly illustrative of the naturalness with which the aggressively secular view is held to be universally applicable. Danish and Norwegian journalists argued that the freedom of the press is absolute, and defamation, ridicule and vilification of religion is in fact exactly what freedom of the press is about – if people react by calling this blasphemous, it just shows how they stick to religious taboos that need to be attacked *qua* taboos. Nothing is holy, they argued; the claim that anything is holy underlines that the religious claim exceptions for themselves. Who is to decide on holiness? The religions? They thereby grant themselves privileges that prevent attacks and criticism.

The significance of this line of argument is very important, for it is a perfect illustration of Ratzinger's point that an intolerant secularism which is common in some European countries now places itself everywhere as the defender of human rights and democracy; in fact, as the very standard that other, less developed, states must follow. Further, this secular hegemony in Europe appropriates human rights to itself by defining freedom of expression in its own intolerant and disrespectful way – it becomes an absolute human right which is exercised in the most free manner when the insult and ridicule of religion is at its height; like an index, the more insulted the religion the more free was the expression.

This is of course pure nonsense and has nothing to do with anything but primitive tastelessness. Freedom of expression is very wide – total in legal terms in many

European states – but that does not mean that it is meant as a channel for all kinds of insulting statements. It is in fact incumbent on the one who expresses himself to take both freedom of religion and the right to one's good name and reputation into account – two of the other fundamental human rights. Further, respect for religions is implied by religious freedom. All this is commonsensical in most European states, but it was noteworthy that in this case both the Nordic states in question as well as the French with a secular tradition had a strong group of spokespersons for an unfettered freedom of speech in the manner described above.

The concept of freedom that underlies the argument for total freedom to express anything, especially that which insults, is also necessarily limitless. Ratzinger correctly identifies this limitless freedom as the major problem with modern democracy. Freedom is not limited by evil deeds when the concept of evil is a subjective one, and doing harm to others is likewise subjective.

The lack of a willingness to delimit this modern freedom ultimately lies in the inability to define the human being: what is good and what is bad about human nature. The Universal Declaration of Human Rights of 1948 does rest on a view of the human being, albeit an implicit one: for instance, in order to live a dignified life, man must be able to enjoy civil and political rights, to have religious space and space and help for his family, etc. If we look carefully, we can delineate the anthropology underlying this declaration. The various human rights form a carefully balanced edifice, and perversions will occur if one right is made absolute.

To return to the previous example, it serves to illustrate how one human right has come to assume a dominant position vis-à-vis other rights. Muslims are not used to having their religion ridiculed, and therefore react with all kinds of unacceptable means, such as violent attacks and threats. No one defends such methods. But if we disregard the unacceptable methods, we see that there is a parallel between the ridicule of

Muslims and Christians in parts of the Western press: Christians are routinely attacked in their own national press, perhaps especially in the Nordic states, but have grown used to it. Nonetheless this development shows that the human right to religious freedom is not respected in our societies – it conflicts head-on with the secular premise that all can and should be ridiculed, and that nothing can be sacred and therefore exempt from this. Those who believe in God will not tolerate blasphemy and can never regard it indifferently, although Christians will tackle this very differently from many Jews and Muslims, given the Christian view of forgiveness. But that is not the point here. The important logical issue is that blasphemy can only make sense to someone with respect for the religious phenomenon, and the right to demand such respect is implicit in the existence of the human right to religious freedom. There either has to be a balance between freedom of speech and freedom of religion in a society, or there will be a clash where one right will attempt to suppress the other. The former was clearly the intention of the framers of the declaration.

This example brings us to the key question of human nature and human rights: the religious need and sense of the holy. Only because the human being has the nature of needing God and seeking God, is there a human right to religious freedom. In writing out this human right the drafters of the declaration have accepted that they thereby affirm something substantial about the human being. Atheists will deny the religious need in man, and here we see that the debate about human rights is really a debate about human nature, just as Charles Malik stated when he commented upon differences between the drafters of the declaration at its inception.

Can there be any other solution to such conflicts other than those based on power? Can freedom be delineated in a rational way? In short, can there be a rationality that is common to all human beings in a society?

This is the question which has preoccupied Ratzinger for many years and which permeates his writings on democracy, human rights and relativism. Few if any contemporary thinkers have pondered this issue with more precision and incision. The criticism of the relative character of the contemporary rationalist paradigm is the starting point. There are few in Europe – as evidenced by the case of the Muhammad drawings – that have discovered that their own paradigm has its flaws.

A Rationality that Embraces Ethics?

The current paradigm of rationality is based on the idea that rationality (*Vernuft*) is independent of both creator and human being. This is, underlines Raztinger, entirely true when we speak about natural science: 'rationality is today limited to the technical area only'.[5] The consequence of accepting only this limited form of rationality is that the human being no longer has any idea of how to reason about right and wrong, and that he has no standard of ethics outside himself: 'the human being no longer recognizes any moral authority outside himself'.[6] This implies that all that is not within the confines of empirical science – all that which relates to political and personal norms and values – is seen as wholly subjective.

Why is this a problem? The difference between a pluralist society and a relativist one lies in the existence of some common norms, *Grundrechte* in German. Citizens are expected to agree on some things, usually thought about as a 'social contract' by political philosophers. For instance, stealing is wrong and must be punished; stable families are good for the upbringing of future citizens and hence good for society, etc. But modern relativism denies any common norms beyond those of political correctness. Indeed, this paradigm leads to a limitless concept of freedom since there are no standards or limits

5   Ibid., p. 52.
6   Ibid.

outside subjective judgement: 'the concept of freedom grows without limits'.[7]

Modern European man has cut off his historical roots and regards history and its philosophical insights as invalid for him. The real progress in natural science has led to the misunderstanding that a similar progress has taken place in human 'science'. Not only is modern man totally ignorant of his own philosophical and theological history, but he believes – tragically – that technical and economic progress implies civilizational progress. Also, the state of technical knowledge dictates what one in fact does with and for the human being, because 'what you know, you are also entitled to do – duty apart from ability to do someting no longer exists'.[8] *Durfen* – the 'should' – the normative question of ethics – is now regarded as something to be resolved by the power of public opinion and personal preference.

Ratzinger concludes his diagnostic: is functional rationality enough for the human being and for politics? The answer is no. Is this rationality self-sufficient? No, when it is used to decide in non-technical matters, i.e. normative ones.

How can rationality be defined beyond the sphere of technical scientific argument? Can there be a rational determination of basic norms and values? This latter question would seem to be a folly today, even if human rights as a concept are based on the postulate of a human nature that is the cause of human rights: we have human rights because we have human *dignity*, as each and every preamble to human rights conventions reads. Further, the Nuremberg trials were premised on the existence of a higher moral law that in fact was argued to be *common* to all human beings and *knowable* for all human beings. If we accept this on purely pragmatic grounds – i.e. the human rights edifice is based on this postulate – we must immediately ask about this form of rationality – does it exist, how does it work?

---

[7]   Ibid., p. 52.
[8]   Ibid., p. 53.

Politics is the Sphere of the Rational

It is very interesting, but not surprising, that Professor Ratzinger as Pope Benedict XVI has chosen to write large parts of his first encyclical about rationality. In the second part of *Deus caritas est*[9] he discusses how rational decisions in political life can be restored. Reason needs constant correction, he states, because 'it can never be free of the danger of a certain ethical blindness caused by the dazzling effect of power and special interests'.[10] Reason is inborn in man, but can be and is often corrupted. This is the ancient Aristotelian position where virtue and vice are in constant contestation. The Church stands firmly in this tradition of natural law, which is not specifically Christian at all. The only role for the Church in political life, says the Pope, is therefore to argue 'on the basis of reason and natural law', 'to help purify reason and to contribute to the acknowledgement and attainment of what is just'.[11]

It is because the Church is 'an expert in humanity' that she has something to contribute in this respect, and the Church 'has to play her part through rational argument'.[12] The aim is to reawaken a sense of justice in people, which is the essence of rational argument about politics. Justice is one of the four cardinal virtues and the one proper to politics in the writings of classical political philosophy. The Pope distinguishes very sharply between the role of religion and that of politics, stating that 'the formation of just

---

[9] This encyclical is addressed to Catholics, not to all 'people of good will'. It is thus an 'internal' document for the Church which adresses the role of the Church in the world. It is highly significant that the Church to non-belivers can and should only be a contributor to society's political debate on secular terms, thus sharply distingusihing between the society of believers – the *Internlogik* of the Church; and its external role in secular society, where it can only act and argue in natural law, secular terms.

[10] Ibid., p. 28.

[11] Ibid.

[12] Ibid.

structures is not the direct duty of the Church, but belongs to the sphere of politics, *the sphere of the autonomous use of reason'*.[13]

The Church should concern herself with souls and with promoting the truth about human nature – its virtues and vices, its ability for improvement; in short, its spiritual life. But politics is something else, an autonomous sphere which is neither religious nor private, but which has its own 'mandate' and rationality. The Pope defines politics as the 'sphere of the autonomous use of reason' – not as that of interests or power, but as the sphere of reason.

How can this be? What does this mean?

In his speech to the Benedictine monastery in Subiaco, on his receipt of the Premio San Benedetto in April 2005 – a few days before he was elected Pope – he underlined that Christianity is the 'religion of the *Logos*'.[14] *Logos* is the Greek word for reason, in Latin *ratio*. To be rational is, surprisingly enough, equivalent to being human: the definition in the classical Aristotelian and Platonic philosophic tradition is that the human being is a 'rational and social animal'. As discussed in previous chapters, rationality is the ability to offer arguments and justifications for something; unlike animals, which also have language and can communicate with each other, the human being is the only entity that can reason about things. Thus, animals fight, make love, procreate, hunt, eat, play and live a communal existence by instinct, but only humans can reason about all these natural activities.

Morever, *ratio* defines the human being itself; without reasoning he simply would not be a human being. The ability to reason is inborn in every human being, but it can be destroyed, such as in illess or handicap, and it can be corrupted, such as in people who refuse to discern right from wrong. Having the *ability* to reason is not equivalent to using that ability.

[13]   Ibid., p. 29, my emphasis.
[14]   Ibid., p. x.

Ratio enables man to reason about fact as well as value: one can discern truth and falsehood in a factual statement, such as 'the house is red'. Unless one is colour blind, one is able to tell whether this is a true statement or not if one knows the word for 'red' and 'house'. But the same logical ability is present in ethical or moral judgements: an uncorrupted human being can arrive at the conclusion that is it wrong to steal or to kill. The much later criticism by David Hume simply misses the point, because the Aristotelian definition of the human being and his rationality entails ethical ability: reasoning about ethics is as natural and inborn, and as rational, as is reasoning about empirically observable facts. Animals will most probably steal each others' prey if they have the chance, whereas humans may do the same and indeed often do, but they nonetheless know that this is wrong. At least they do not believe that it is right.

The modern European rationality is therefore only a partial rationality, as it extends only to technical, mathematical, or empirical knowledge. The entire classical tradition of humanism has been forgotten and suppressed over centuries of scepticism and criticism such as Hume's. One may object that this tradition has thereby been rendered obsolete by most modern standards, and that it cannot be revived and made usable to the modern, secular human being.

Reviving Natural Law

It must first be said that the natural law tradition is by no means religiously founded. It is an entirely secular tradition that postulates one premise, viz. that there is a knowable and constant human nature, and that knowledge is arrived at through rational discernment. The Pope, when he was still cardinal, made the point to me in conversations that natural law has to be re-made in modern language; its premises are valid, but one cannot revive a tradition that has been sidelined for so many centuries as it had been.[15] Certainly natural law as applied to the natural sciences has lost its validity.

However, in the field of values or norms, natural law thinking has persisted, especially in Catholic philosophy and in the Church itself. In previous chapters in this book I have spent a lot of time showing the absurdity of a totally relativist position, and it is easy to refute such a position. As we have seen, both human rights and democracy are upheld by relativists as ethically right and good, thus creating the paradox that the West proclaims relativism in all things ethical but not in the area of political governance. The contradiction in terms that is evident in the area of human rights is clear: human rights cannot exist as a concept, even less as a reality, if they are based on a relativist position.

The defining characteristic of the human being is *ratio*, and as the Pope points out, Christianity is the religion of the *Logos*, of *ratio*. All things concerning ethics can therefore be discerned by what is often referred to as 'right reason', that is, uncorrupted reason. Natural law, which is the term St Thomas Aquinas uses for the ethics of man's life in the city, of political life, is entirely accessible to the human mind. Faith as such is even accessible by reason, as evidenced in his logical proof of the existence of God. Today this proof is less popular and esteemed, but I mention it simply to underline how far human reason is credited in the Catholic tradition.

St Thomas took his knowledge and inspiration directly from Aristotle, via the long 'detour' of Arab philosophy. If we look at the Aristotelian notion of man, we find the word *ousia* which means 'substrate', something which is in and of itself, underlying all things that change. In Latin, this term is rendered *substantia*, substance. *Essentia*, essence, is another expression of this. Genus and other characteristics are 'accidents', accidental, but the human being is essence, primary and universal.

---

[15] Private conversations and correspondence, 2003–2005.

The definition of the human being as 'being' is therefore that it is an entity that is not derived from anything else; it is the most primary substance, along with other natural creatures such as animals. Aristotle is an empiricist in the sense that he proceeds by observation and classification based on this: he therefore observes that both men and animals are social beings, but that only man is a rational being even if animals also have language, as stated above.

This classical postulate, the definition of the human being by his rational faculty, was adopted by philosophers and theologians in the early Middle Ages and later, as mentioned, rediscovered by St Thomas Aquinas. For instance, in the sixth century Boethius states that man is a '*rationalis naturae individua substantia*', 'an individual substance of a rational nature'[16] and the Stoics of the later Stoa in Rome all postulated the rational ability of man in ethical matters as the important characteristic. The ability to discern and to do the right things was termed 'virtue', the Latin for manly, strong, derived as it is from the word for man, *vir*. The cardinal virtues were known and practised throughout antiquity, from Socrates' quest for justice in the Platonic dialogues to Marcus Aurelius' commentaries on how to practise fortitude and temperance in the governing of the Roman Empire.

The human being, then, is created with rationality, and indeed this quality is what distinguishes him from animals. The virtues are the characteristics of human nature that allow man to develop, and the corresponding vices are the ways to become less human, to de-humanize oneself. In Aristotelian ontology all beings have a purpose, a *telos*, and the purpose of the human being is to perfect the virtues and combat the vices. This is so crucial that it is intrinsic to him in the sense that being itself is 'more or less' according to how virtuous a person is. A vile person has less reality or being than a virtuous man, and we recognize a remnant of this in the expression 'de-human-

---

[16] Contra Eutychen, III, 6.

ization' which we use for someone who is really vile. To the relativist this language cannot logically make sense, as virtue and vice are but subjective preferences. Yet people still realize what de-humanization means; someone who is 'less than' human.

The *telos* of man is *eudemonia,* happiness, but this is not in the sense of pleasures and indulgences, but in the sense of self-discipline, justice, prudence, and temperance. According to the ancient precept, only the person who fully masters himself is happy. It is said that emperor Marcus Aurelius lived an ascetic and frugal life, a Spartan existence, in order to conquer his passions – among which sexual passion is probably the least important. The ingredients in ethical living were known very precisely: the virtues were all interconnected; parameters whereby one would navigate in everyday life, and vices could only be combated through strength, i.e. virtue. In the Stoic universe detachment from life's vicissitudes and temptations played a key role, as did the practice of being ready for death. 'Death frees the soul from its envelope', Marcus Aurelius said. Not fearing death gave strength, perspective on life, and the ability to appreciate the here and now in real terms.

When we look at Christian teaching, we rediscover the same elements, this time with an addition of supernatural virtue – the theological ones of faith, hope, and charity. In Christianity the ancient programme of character formation continues: one must acquire natural virtues before one can aspire to attain the supernatural ones. In the famous dictum of St Thomas Aquinas, 'faith builds on nature and perfects it'. There is no point in trying to be a good Christian unless one is prepared to be a good human being; it is simply an impossibility, for divine virtue cannot be attained by a vile person. Forgiveness can of course be dispensed at the discretion of the Lord, but virtue is like an edifice built stone by stone.

What happened to the classical scheme of character formation? Why did people stop believing in the objective truth of virtue and vice, and in human nature itself? This is of course the long story of refutations of metaphysics since the late Renaissance, but it is in many ways a story that is correct and progressive regarding natural science, but which is not so regarding ethics. As Professor Rattinger points out, the old precepts of natural law with regard to natural science have been refuted and justly discarded, but this development is not correct with regard to ethics. There has been no Copernican revolution with regard to progress in defining human nature, only a long row of sceptical philosophers who have dispensed with the concept altogether.

Why do we Think that Human Nature Cannot be Defined?

While natural science progressed, human science, or the *Geisteswissenschaften*, did not. However, the classical definition of the human being and his nature, and the formative need for cultivating virtue, was upheld as the essence of European *Bildung* for many centuries. In the words of Italian philosophy professor Enrico Berti, 'It remained the basis of global culture, not only Christian but also Jewish and Muslim, both ancient, mediaeval, and modern, that is of the entire culture which Aristotelian tradition has influenced; indeed, we find variations in Augustine, John Damascene, Richard of St Victor, Thomas Aquinas, Leibnitz, Rosmini, Maritain and several other thinkers'.[17]

But with the advent of natural science followed a 'spillover' to metaphysics. From the time of John Locke we see that his notion of the person cannot yield natural law, although he writes in the natural law tradition. For Locke, the human being cannot be known or defined because it cannot be arrived at through direct sense experience.

---

[17] E. Berti, 'The Classical Notion of Person in Today's Philosophical Debate', paper presented at the Papal Academy of Social Science, annual conference, September 2005.

The human being is something other than mere sensation, Locke thinks, but because he cannot sense it or observe it, it must remain unknown. This line of thought is developed further by Berkeley who argues that 'being is preception' (*esse est percipi*) and reaches it high point (or low point, as it were) in the empiricism of David Hume.

Hume does away with metaphysics altogether, but he also does away with physics: his scepticism is such that not even observations of causation count as causation: If we see a ball hitting another ball, all that we observe are two sequential occurrences – and that observation does not allow us to infer that the first ball *caused* the other to roll when hitting it. Hume argues that since we have seen this before, we expect the first ball to make the other roll, but this is simply a habit of ours. Since we can never *observe* the concept of cause, we can never know anything about it! On this ontology, there is no ontology, even less human nature that can be known – all that exists is a series of sense experiences. Since we cannot observe ourselves, only notice our own behaviour, we have no substance or identity, all that we can know about ourselves is a series of disconnected sense experiences. In justice to Hume I should mention that he found his own philosophy entirely dissatisfactory,[18] but declared that science could not help.

At this point we are faced with the delineation of the concept of science and also rationality to natural science alone. Only that which can be empirically observed and proven can exist scientifically. While this is true for natural science, it has however never been true for the human sciences. The reductionism of science to natural science leaves metaphysics dead and philosophy ill at ease; now condemned to dealing with lesser questions than ontology and epistemology. It no longer makes sense to study the major questions of ethics when one

---

[18] See Appendix, David Hume, *Treatise of Human Nature*.

cannot deal with the premises of ethics by meaningfully asking what human nature is like and how it can fulfil its goals.

Immanuel Kant tries to 'rescue' objective human nature by postulating it *a priori*, like an axiom of mathematics. The human being is a rational being endowed with dignity, he postulates, and therefore should not be treated as an object, a means, but as an end in itself. But praise-worthy as this may be, Kant's postulate remains but a postulate since nothing about human nature can be known. The ethics, or moral imperative, are necessary because otherwise men would become utilitarian beasts.

Later, in the nineteenth century, Hegel and Fichte further destroy the notion of metaphysics, denying that essences can exist and be known: all is idea, nothing is real. And after that we find that the concept of different cultures replace human nature: the person is a 'product' of culture and society in both Marxism and modern anthro-pology. Relativism has become the very premise.

The impossibility of objective reality – sometimes dubbed *essentialism* – is further developed by analytical language philosophy which argues that reality cannot exist apart from language itself; it is in fact constituted by language. This school of thought is present today in the pervasive approach called constructivism in the social and human sciences: political reality, especially norms, is socially constructed. Likewise, the positivist turn in legal philosophy which underlies most European legal thought denies that there is any reality to the concept of justice: the law is what the letter of the law says.

However, given this, there is now a turn back to meta-physics in important schools of philosophy: in the Oxford and Cambridge schools of ordinary language philosophy there is a return to the classical concept of the person.[19] In his famous book *Word and Object*, the American philosopher W. O. Quine argues that language must refer to objects which in turn give meaning to language – i.e. it is the objects that exist independently and language that describes them, not the other way round, as constructivism and analytic language philosophy would have it.

In the continental tradition we also find very significant objections to the death of metaphysics in personalism and hermeneutics. Personalist philosophers like Jonas, Mounier, Ricoeur, and the late Pope John Paul II have emphazised that the experience of the other provides the basis for knowledge of human nature and ethics. Mounier himself states that the classical concept of person 'is the best candidate to sustain legal, political, economic and social battles in defence of human rights'.[20] The reason for this is entirely simple and logical: if equality is the central notion of law and politics, then this implies that there is something knowable about the human person that is the same everywhere and always. This is also the central point of my argument that human rights are a natural law concept – they demand and presuppose one common human nature in terms of the same dignity and the same equality.

Natural Law Today: Where is the Evidence?

So far we have merely shown that for many centuries the Western philosophical tradition upheld the classical notion of human nature as 'rational and social', and that metaphysics was sidelined, first by British empiricism which equated the human and the natural sciences, and later by increasingly sceptical strands of thought. However, much of the problem with this evolution in the history of philosophy had to do with the immense progress in empirical and natural science and the deplorable lack of such in the human sciences. But it also has to do with the confusion between the two, premised

---

[19]   I am indebted to Enrico Berti's paper, op. cit., for the remainder of this analysis.

[20]   Berti, op. cit., p. 10.

on the paradigm that human science must imitate natural science in order to progress.

None of this has disproved Aristotle. The argument remains that the human being can reason about ethics as he can reason about facts. The Humean criticism misses the point when it faults Aristotle with confusing 'fact and values', for the classical concept postulates that the person is both 'fact and value' in its very essence – being rational means being ethical. This point is the most foreign of all to modern man, and the very unfortunate separation of the two that Hume made has henceforth obscured the possibility of natural law.

Let us now give natural law a chance, as it were. Could Aristotle be right? In an interesting paper the Swedish MP Per Landgren records an imaginary incidence.[21]

Two people rescue people from a burning house. They are subsequently interviewed by the press, and a journalist asks why they risked their own lives to do this. One says that he did not think about that question at all; he simply acted. But the other says that he thought that he would become rich from getting a prize for valour, that he could get famous, etc. The journalist is puzzled over this answer. Something seems very wrong, undignified, and unnatural about it.

This example illustrates the argument which natural law makes: a *natural* reaction is to try to save life, even if one is afraid. An *unnatural* reaction is to do it to make money from it. One may even say that the latter reaction is evil, bad, wrong – thus, there is a *natural* ability in us to discern right from wrong.

Further, saving life – one's own and that of others – seems to be a basic value, whereas the need to make money can be many things, and varies between being a vital and good thing when one must provide for one's family, and being a bad thing when a person saves life in

---

[21] Per Landgren, 'Naturretten – en mansklig etikk', ch. 5, *Det gemensamma basta – Om kristdemokratiens idegrund*, Stockholm, 2002.

order to make money, as in the example above. Thus, ethics makes sense only in a context of *telos*, as Aristotle argues.

Landgren makes the point that there are some basic values which are universally recognized as such: to live rather than to die, to be respected, to be healthy, to learn, to cherish truth rather than lies, etc.[22] The opposite of these values are morbid and unnatural, most people would immediately agree. These basic values are called 'intrinsic', 'Grundwerte', 'Rechtsguter'.[23]

The point about these values is that they are inborn, intrinsic, constitutive – they define what a human being is, just like Aristotle's definition. This is so because we cannot derive them from any principles or logical arguments; they are simply what human beings, *grosso modo*, are like. True, there are mass murderers and masochists around, but we tend to describe them as aberrations, perversions, unnaturals. If we were true relativists, we would have to say that a mass murderer just has another subjective preference from ours.

Thus, when we read the Universal Declaration of Human Rights, we see that the rights therein are largely such basic principles that are commonsensical to all reasonable persons. Reasonable means, we recall, that one is upright and human; not corrupted and evil. And the author of this human nature, creator or not, does not have to be mentioned, but the rights form a whole that reflect a view of human nature which is knowable through common sense and reason. But if the concept of human nature is denied, there is no basis for these human rights – they become mere ideological and political devices. Human nature remains an axiom, as it was also to Aristotle, an essence and prime mover, as he would have called it.

But it remains fully possible to discern what human dignity and therefore human rights is about through the

---

[22]   Landgren, op. cit., p. 120.
[23]   Ibid.

faculty of reason, deductive as well as inductive. The sharpness of the rational mind is a function of its ascetic and logical training, both in terms of consistent argument – 'If all men are equal, one man cannot be discriminated' – and ethics – 'If stealing is wrong, I must refrain from it lest my ethical sense be dulled.' The problem, I think, lies not so much in lack of reason as in lack of virtue. It is rather easy to know what is right and wrong, but rather arduous and unpleasant to do what is right. As a Catholic dictum puts it, tongue-in-cheek: 'A little virtue does not hurt you, but vice is nice.'

In conclusion, the relativist position is untenable and the rationalist position is possible. There is no need to discard Aristotle's ontology, the classical notion of the person, and mere logic itself demands that the law be concerned with universals, not with subjective interests. But it remains a tall order indeed to restore rationality to Western politics.

BIBLIOGRAPHY

Abbott, K.W. and Snidal, D., 'Hard and Soft Law in International Governance', *International Organization*, 54, 3, summer 2000.

Abbott, K.W. et al., 'The Concept of Legalization', *International Organization*, 54, 3, summer 2000.

Annuario Pontificio, 1999, Vatican City State.

Chayes, A. and Chayes, A., *The New Sovereignty: Compliance with International Regulatory Agreements*, Harvard University Press, 1995.

Convention for the Protection of Human Rights and Fundamental Freedoms: Council of Europe, ets. no. 5, Rome 4.11.1950.

Cortrell, A. and Davis, J.W., 'How Do International Institutions Matter? The Domestic Impact of International Norms and Rules', *International Studies Quarterly*, 40, 1996, pp. 451-478.

Donnelly, J., 'State Sovereignty and International Intervention: The Case of Human Rights', in Lyons, op. cit., 1995.

Donnelly, J., 'Human Rights: The Impact of International Action', *International Journal*, XLIII, spring 1988.

Draft Charter of Fundamental Rights of the EU, Brussels, 16 May 2000.

DUPI (Danish Foreign Policy Institute), *Humanitær intervention. Retlige og politiske aspekter*, Copenhagen, 1999 (no specific authors: study presented by DUPI itself).

Emberland, M., 'Er det legitimt å tolke EMKG dynamisk?', conference paper, University of Oslo, 2006.

Finnemore, M., 'Constructing Norms of Humanitarian Intervention', in Katzenstein, op. cit., 1996.

Finnemore, M., *National Interests in International Society*, Cornell University Press, Ithaca, 1996.

Finnemore, M. and Sikkink, K., 'International Norm Dynamics and Political Change', *International Organization*, 52, 4, autumn 1998.

Flynn, G. and Farrell, H., 'Piecing Together the Democratic Peace: The CSCE, Norms, and the "Construction" of Security in Post-Cold War Europe', *International Organization*, 53, 3, summer 1999.

Fox, G.H., 'New Approaches to International Human Rights: The Sovereign State Revisited', in Hasmi, S., op. cit., 1997.

Glendon, M.A., *A World made New: Eleanor Roosevelt and the Universal Declaration of Human Rights*, Alfred Knoph, New York., 2001.

Goldmann, K., 'The Line in Water: International and Domestic Politics', *Cooperation and Conflict*, XXIV, 1989.

Glendon, M.A., *Rights Talk: The Impoverishment of Political Discourse*, The Free Press, New York, 1991.

Glendon, M.A., 'Knowing the Universal Declaration of Human Rights', *Notre Dame Law Review*, 75, 5, 1998.

Goldstein, J., 'Introduction: Legalization and World Politics', *International Organization*, 54, 3, summer 2000.

Gourevitch, P., 'The second image reversed: the international sources of domestic politics', *International Organization*, 32, 4, 1978.

Gow, J., 'Shared Sovereignty, Enhanced Security: lessons from the Yuogoslav War', in Hasmi, S., op. cit., 1997.

Haas, P.M., 'Introduction: Epistemic Communities and international policy coordination', *International Organization*, 46, 1, winter 1992.

Haas, P.M., 'Epistemic Communities and the Dynamics of International Environmental Cooperation', in Rittberger, op. cit., 1993.

Haufler, V., 'Crossing the Boundary between Public and Private: International Regimes and Non-State Actors', in Rittberger, op. cit., 1993.

Hopkins, R., 'The International Role of "domestic" bureaucracy', *International Organization*, 30, 3, 1976.

Hurd, I., 'Legitimacy and Authority in International Politics', *International Organization*, 53, 2, spring 1999.

Ingebritsen, C., 'Scandinavia's Influence on International Norms: The Cases of Environment, Security, and Welfare', unpublished paper, 1999?

Kahler, M., 'Rationality in International Relations', *International Organization*, 52, 4, autumn 1998.

Kahler, M., 'Conclusion: The Causes and Consequences of Legalization', *International Organization*, 54, 3, summer 2000.

Kamarck, E.C. and Nye, J., *democracy.com? Goverance in a Networked World*, Hollis Publishing Company, Hollis, 1999.

Keck, M. and Sikkink, K., *Activists beyond Borders. Advocacy Networks in International Politics*, Cornell University Press, Ithaca, New York, 1998.

Keohane, R., 'Empathy and International Regimes', in Mansbridge, op. cit., 1990.

Keohane, R. et al., 'Legalized Dispute Resolution: Interstate and Transnational', *International Organization*, 54, 3, summer 2000.

Klotz, A., 'Norms reconstituting interests: global racial equality and US sanctions against South Africa', *International Organization*, 49, 3, summer 1995.

Koh, H., 'Why Do Nations Obey International Law?', *Yale Law Review*, 106, 8, June 1997.

Krasner, S., *Sovereignty: Organized Hypocrasy*, Princeton University Press, Princeton, New Jersey, 1999.

Lyons, G. and Mastanduno, M., 'Introduction: International Intervention, State Sovereignty, and the Future of International Society', in Lyons, G. and Mastanduno, H. (eds) *Beyond Westphalia: State Sovereignty and International Intervention*, Johns Hopkins University Press, Baltimore, 1995.

Matláry, J.H., *Soft Power, Hard Values: The Impact of Democratic Norms in Europe*, Macmillan, Houndmills, Basingstoke, 2001.

Nye, J., *Bound to Lead: The Changing Nature of American Power*, Basic Books, New York, 1995.

Nye, J., 'Redefining the National Interest', *Foreign Affairs,* 78, 4, July/August, 1999.

Nye, J. and Owens, W. 'America's Information Edge', *Foreign Affairs,* March/April 1996.

Pontifical Council for Justice and Peace, *The Social Agenda: A Collection of Magisterial Texts,* edited by Fr Marciel Zieba, OP and Fr Robert Sirico, Libreria Editrice Vaticana, 2000.

Ratzinger, J., 'Europa in the Krise der Kulturen', acceptance speech for 'Premio san Benedetto' in St Scholastica, Subiaco, on 1 April 2005; published by Cantagalli and Libreria Editrice Vaticana under the same title, 2006.

Risse-Kappen, T., *Bringing Transnational Relations back in: Non-state Actors, Domestic Structures and International Institutions,* Cambridge University Press, Cambridge, 1995.

Rittberger, V. and Mayer, P., *Regime Theory and International Relations,* Clarendon Press, Oxford, 1993.

Rosas, A., 'The Decline of Sovereignty: Legal Perspectives', in Iivonen, J. (ed.) *The Future of the Nation State in Europe,* Aldershot, UK, 1993.

Rosas, A., 'State Sovereignty and Human Rights: Towards a Global Constitutional Project', *Political Studies,* XLIII, 1995.

Rosenau, J.N. and Czempiel, E.-O., (eds) *Governance without Government: Order and Change in World politics,* Cambridge Studies in International Relations, Cambridge, 1992.

Rosenau, J.N. and Czempiel, E.-O., 'Sovereignty in a Turbulent World', in Lyons, op. cit., 1995.

Ruggie, J.G. (ed.), *Multilateralism Matters. The Theory and Praxis of an Institutional Form,* Columbia University Press, New York, 1993.

Ruggie, J.G., 'What Makes the World Hang Together? Neo-Utilitarianism and the Social Constructivist Challenge', *International Organization,* 1992.

Sikkink, K., 'The Power of Principled Ideas: Human Rights Policies in the US and Europe', in Goldstein, J. and

Keohane, R. (eds) *Ideas and Foreign Policy: Beliefs, Institutions, and Political Change*, Cornell University Press, Ithaca and London, 1993.

Slaughter, A.-M., 'International Law in a World of Liberal States', *European Journal of International Law*, 6, 4, 1995.

Tarzi, S., 'The Role of Norms and Regimes in World Affairs: A Grotian Perspective', *International Relations*, XIV, 3, 1998.

Thomas, D.C., 'The Helsinki Accords and Political Change in Eastern Europe', in Risse et al. (eds), *The Power of Human Rights. International Norms and Domestic Change*, Cambridge University Press, Cambridge, 1999.

Universal Declaration of Human Rights, 1948.

Weigel, G., *The Final Revolution. The Resistance Church and the Collapse of Communism*, Oxford University Press, Oxford, 1992.

Weigel, G., Witness to Hope. *The Biography of John Paul II*, HaperCollins, New York, 1999.

Weiler, J.H.H., 'European Neo-Constitutionalism: in search of foundations for the European Consitutional Order', in Bellamy, R. and Castiglione, D. (eds), *Constitutionalism in Transformation: European and Theoretical Perspectives*, Blackwell, Oxford, 1996.

Weiler, J.H.H., *The Constitution of Europe: Do the new Clothes have an Emperor?'*, Cambridge University Press, Cambridge, 1999.